BEYOND GROWTH HACKING

MANAGING INNOVATION IN BUSINESS STRATEGY, MARKETING AND FINANCE

Series Editors:

Stefano Bresciani – University of Turin, Italy
Antonio Salvi – University of Turin, Italy
Amandeep Dhir – University of Agder, Norway
Alberto Ferraris – University of Turin, Italy

At the centre of this series is the goal to contribute to understanding the role of business innovation from the perspective of three key functional areas: strategy, marketing and finance. With individual titles applying this goal to large businesses, small businesses, family businesses and more, the reader is given unique insight into the interplay of innovation in strategy, marketing and finance.

Contributions provide an innovative and enriching perspective on the newest trends in innovation management and the developmental barriers it can create. Furthermore, the volumes provide insights into modern social media usage in enterprises and the impact on consumers' well-being, sustainable competitiveness in the business and finance context. Books in this series are of value to researchers, academics, professionals and students in the fields of management, finance and business strategy.

BEYOND GROWTH HACKING: MASTERING BUSINESS MODEL EVOLUTION

BY

GABRIELE SANTORO
University of Turin, Italy, and University of Nicosia, Cyprus

AND

AUGUSTO BARGONI
University of Turin, Italy

United Kingdom – North America – Japan – India
Malaysia – China

Emerald Publishing Limited
Emerald Publishing, Floor 5, Northspring, 21-23 Wellington Street, Leeds LS1 4DL.

First edition 2025

Copyright © 2025 Gabriele Santoro and Augusto Bargoni.
Published under exclusive licence by Emerald Publishing Limited.

Reprints and permissions service
Contact: www.copyright.com

No part of this book may be reproduced, stored in a retrieval system, transmitted in any form or by any means electronic, mechanical, photocopying, recording or otherwise without either the prior written permission of the publisher or a licence permitting restricted copying issued in the UK by The Copyright Licensing Agency and in the USA by The Copyright Clearance Center. No responsibility is accepted for the accuracy of information contained in the text, illustrations or advertisements. The opinions expressed in these chapters are not necessarily those of the Author or the publisher.

British Library Cataloguing in Publication Data
A catalogue record for this book is available from the British Library

ISBN: 978-1-83608-443-3 (Print)
ISBN: 978-1-83608-442-6 (Online)
ISBN: 978-1-83608-444-0 (Epub)

Printed and bound by CPI Group (UK) Ltd, Croydon, CR0 4YY

INVESTOR IN PEOPLE

CONTENTS

About the Authors   vii

Introduction   1

1   Before to Begin: Modelling the Business   3
    1.1.   Business Model. An Architecture for Understanding the Organisation   4
       1.1.1.   The Business Model Canvas   6
       1.1.2.   Lean Canvas   9
    1.2.   Business Model Dynamics   11
       1.2.1.   Business Model Validation   14
       1.2.2.   Business Model Scaling   14
       1.2.3.   Business Model Innovation   15
       1.2.4.   Business Model Pivot   15

2   Digital Business Models   17
    2.1.   An Introduction to Digital Ecosystems   18
    2.2.   Platforms as Digital Ecosystems   19
    2.3.   Business Models of Platforms: Features and Issues   20
       2.3.1.   Clearly Define the Various Sides of the Market   23
       2.3.2.   Define Your Own Unique Value Proposition and Business Model   23
       2.3.3.   Stimulate Direct and Indirect Network Effects, If Any   24
       2.3.4.   Solve the Chicken-or-Egg Problem   25
       2.3.5.   Explore Opportunities for Scope   27
       2.3.6.   Define Precise Governance Mechanisms   28

3	Defining Growth Hacking	31
	3.1. First Wave: Unprecedented Growth Through Resource Leveraging	32
	3.2. Second Wave: From GH to Growth	40
	3.3. Design Thinking, Lean Start-up, Agile, and GH	50
	3.3.1. Design Thinking	50
	3.3.2. Lean Start-up	52
	3.3.3. Agile	54
	3.3.4. Growth Hacking	56
	3.3.5. Integrating the Methodologies	58
4	Practising Growth	63
	4.1. Strategic Management. Defining the Path Forward	63
	4.2. Ryan Holiday's Four Growth Steps	69
	4.2.1. Product–Market Fit	69
	4.2.2. Finding the 'Hack'	70
	4.2.3. Harnessing Virality	72
	4.2.4. Data-driven Customer Retention	74
	4.3. Pirate Funnel	76
	4.4. OKRs-driven Growth	81
	4.5. The Experimentation Process	83
	4.6. Organising the Team	87
	4.6.1. The Growth Team	88
5	Growth and Business Model Dynamics	91
	5.1. On Scalability and Optimisation/Improvement	92
	5.2. Not All Platforms are Scalable in the Same Way. The Case of Utravel	96
	5.3. Determining the Degree of Scalability	100
6	Factors Driving Growth	103
References		119

ABOUT THE AUTHORS

Gabriele Santoro, PhD in Business and Management, is Associate Professor in Innovation Management and Digital Transformation at the School of Management and Economics, University of Torino. He undertakes research integrated with the Department of Management of the University of Torino; his main areas of research include business model dynamics, growth hacking, digital ecosystems and platforms and open innovation. He has authored/coauthored several papers in international journals such as *Technovation, Technological Forecasting and Social Change, Small Business Economics*, and *Journal of Business Research*. He is currently Associate Editor of *EuroMed Journal of Business* and *Journal of Responsible Production and Consumption*. He is one of the shareholders of Progesia s.r.l.s., a consulting firm based in Turin (Italy). As such, he works as consultant on projects related to e-commerce management, growth hacking strategies, innovation development, and strategy.

Augusto Bargoni, PhD, is Assistant Professor at the Department of Management, University of Turin. He actively contributes to conducting research on the topics of marketing and entrepreneurship. Since 2022, he is Associate Researcher at the European Centre for Business Research, a joint scientific research workplace of Pan-European University in Prague, and the Faculty of Economic and Entrepreneurship of Pan-European University in Bratislava and other associated institutional partners. He is also Associate Fellow of the EuroMed Research Business Institute (Cyprus). He actively publishes scientific articles in international journals and is member of Editorial Boards of indexed academic journals. He is a member of SIM (Società Italiana Marketing) and SIMA (Società Italiana Management). He presents papers to conferences on a European basis.

INTRODUCTION

In an era defined by rapid technological advancements and shifting market landscapes, the agility and innovation capacity of a business are not just assets but prerequisites for sustainable growth. This book, at its core, is a comprehensive guide designed to navigate the ever-changing landscapes of modern business models, digital transformation, and the nuanced dynamics of firm growth. It is structured to provide readers with a deep understanding of the architecture of business models, the principles of digital innovation, and the tactical execution of growth strategies to enhance resilience and boost performance. We begin our journey by laying the foundational knowledge needed to model a business effectively. Drawing upon the latest academic research, we delve into the dynamics of business models, including validation, scaling, innovation, and the ability to pivot – each a critical component in the lifecycle of a business. In fact, there is a general consensus among academics and practitioners that a business model is an architecture of value creation, delivery, and capture mechanisms (Teece, 2010) serving as the blueprint to define the way a company operates, generates revenue, and sustains itself in the market. It appears crucial to specifically understand how value is created and captured (Costa Climent & Haftor, 2021; Foss & Saebi, 2017) by firms in order to understand how businesses function and how they create and sustain a competitive advantage (Ancillai et al., 2023; Massa et al., 2017; Rietveld & Schilling, 2021).

As we progress, the focus shifts to the digital realm, where digital business models are explored. The rapid and continuous technological advancements have made it nearly impossible for companies to solely develop new products and services internally. Modern technological products rely on software and hardware integrations, and modules that are difficult to develop and produce within a single company. This necessitates new open and participatory approaches and ecosystems, sometimes involving collaborations between competitors (Bresciani et al., 2018). We discuss how these models differ from traditional ones and how they provide new avenues for growth and innovation.

Defining growth hacking constitutes a significant portion of this discourse, presenting it not just as a buzzword but as a systematic approach to unprecedented growth (Bargoni et al., 2023; Bargoni, Santoro, et al., 2024; Troisi et al., 2020). We explore its evolution from leveraging resources creatively to becoming a sophisticated strategy that integrates design thinking, lean start-up methodologies, and agile practices (Bargoni, Smrčka, et al., 2024; Maurya, 2022). The practice of growth hacking, a section dedicated to the application of theoretical knowledge, offers insights into strategic management, Ryan Holiday's (2014) growth steps, the pirate funnel, and objectives and key results (OKRs). It also covers the experimentation process and the organisation of teams to foster a culture of growth (Sanasi, 2023).

In addressing growth and business model dynamics, we scrutinise the scalability and optimisation of different platforms, using case studies to illustrate these principles in action. This part of the book is pivotal for understanding that not all platforms scale in the same way and that strategic thinking must be applied to navigate these differences. Finally, we deep dive into the factors driving growth, providing a nuanced perspective on what propels businesses forward in today's competitive environment. This section is intended to equip readers with the knowledge to identify and leverage these drivers in their contexts.

This book is a beacon for entrepreneurs, executives, and students who aspire to understand the intricacies of modern business models and the strategies that drive growth in the digital age. It offers a blend of theoretical frameworks and practical insights, ensuring that readers are well-equipped to navigate the challenges and opportunities that lie ahead.

As we embark on this journey together, let us remember that the path to growth is not linear. It is a journey of learning, adapting, and innovating. Welcome to the exploration of business models, digital transformation, and the art and science of growth hacking.

1

BEFORE TO BEGIN: MODELLING THE BUSINESS

ABSTRACT

This chapter explores the fundamental concept of a business model, which serves as the foundational architecture for understanding how a company operates, generates revenue, and sustains itself in the market. Emphasising the significance of value creation, delivery, and capture, the chapter outlines how a business model functions as a strategic blueprint, highlighting its dynamic nature in response to evolving market conditions and technological advancements. It delves into the necessity of validating, scaling, innovating, and pivoting business models to achieve growth and maintain competitive advantage. Various frameworks, such as the Business Model Canvas and Lean Canvas are introduced as tools for visualising, analysing, and iterating business strategies. These frameworks help entrepreneurs and managers to identify customer needs, design value propositions, and establish sustainable revenue streams. Further discussion includes the concept of business model dynamics, stressing the importance of adaptability and continuous innovation in today's fast-paced business environment. The chapter concludes with how businesses like Amazon, Uber, Netflix, and LinkedIn have successfully employed different business models over time to sustain growth and achieve market leadership. By providing practical examples and strategic insights, this chapter underscores the critical role of business models in fostering innovation, guiding strategic decision-making, and ensuring long-term success in an ever-changing business landscape.

Keywords: Growth hacking; business model innovation; scale up; business model dynamics; management; value creation

1.1. BUSINESS MODEL. AN ARCHITECTURE FOR UNDERSTANDING THE ORGANISATION

Before tackling growth and data-driven models related to experiments, it's essential to understand what a company does, how it does it, and why. In other words, it's necessary to grasp what a business model is and how it functions. The business model is to a company what DNA is to a living organism or the nature of a plant; without understanding it, it's impossible to define how to water it, how much light to provide, and so forth. The first major assumption of this book is that experimental, data-driven methodologies allow not only for the validation and improvement of a business model but also for its growth. As some examples will show, growth and the test-and-learn approach enable the generation and testing of ideas, developing new products and services. Similarly, the nature of the business model has a significant impact on the effectiveness of growth strategies. For example, as we will see throughout the book, business models subject to strong network effects should be supported by referral strategies, in such a way as to increase value for the individual user when they bring in new users. But before delving into the core of the book, let's take a step back to understand what a business model is and what business model dynamics are. This will allow us to shed light on how business objectives (validation, innovation, pivot, and scaling) are necessary to outline growth strategies.

There is a general consensus among academics and practitioners that a business model is an architecture of value creation, delivery, and capture mechanisms (Teece, 2010). It serves as the blueprint to define the way a company operates, generates revenue, and sustains itself in the market. More specifically, value creation and appropriation are conceived as a firm's boundary-spanning activity system, conducted by a set of actors linked by transaction mechanisms (Costa Climent & Haftor, 2021; Foss & Saebi, 2017). Business models are crucial to understand how businesses function and how they create and sustain a competitive advantage (Ancillai et al., 2023; Massa et al., 2017; Rietveld & Schilling, 2021).

Over time, both academic and practitioner-oriented literature has provided various frameworks and models to effectively explain a company's business model. Several studies and practitioners agree that a business model can be explained through three main components:

(1) *Value creation:* It is a concept that lies at the core of every business model. A business identifies a specific need or problem in the market and designs its products or services to address that need. This is the essence of what a business offers to its customers, and it must provide real value to attract and retain them. In other words, value creation is a section of the business model that describes what products and services the company offers, to which target (i.e. customers), and what needs are being satisfied.

(2) *Value delivery:* Once a business has created value through its products or services, it must determine how it will deliver that value to its customers. This involves decisions about distribution channels, marketing strategies, and customer engagement. How a company chooses to reach its target audience plays a crucial role in its success.

(3) *Value capture:* The final piece of the puzzle is value capture, which refers to how a business monetises the value it delivers. This includes revenue generation strategies, pricing models, and income streams. A business must ensure that the value it creates is translated into sustainable financial returns.

Other studies suggest another component to define and explain how a business model works: *value configuration*. It refers to the arrangement and integration of key resources and activities within a business model to effectively create and deliver value to customers. It involves a thoughtful design of how a company's assets, capabilities, and partnerships work together to achieve its strategic goals. This component is especially relevant in the context of platforms, which are often linked to open business models in which resources are often attracted from external parties and activities delegated externally. For example, Uber does not own the cars to transport users. Likewise, drivers are not hired.

Callout 1. Business Model Examples

✓ *Amazon*: Amazon's business model is built on offering a vast selection of products (value proposition) through an efficient online platform (channel) to a global customer base (customer segments). They generate revenue through sales, subscriptions (Amazon Prime), and third-party seller fees.

> ✓ *Uber*: Uber's business model centres around connecting riders and drivers (value proposition) through a mobile app (channel). They earn revenue by taking a percentage of each ride fare (revenue streams).
>
> ✓ *Netflix*: Netflix provides a vast library of streaming content (value proposition) accessible through its platform (channel) to subscribers (customer segments) who pay a monthly fee (revenue streams).
>
> ✓ *LinkedIn*: LinkedIn adopts a 'freemium' business model, attracting customers by introducing them to basic, limited-scope products. Then, with the client using their service, the company attempts to convert them to a more premium, advance product that requires payment. Although a customer may theoretically stay on freemium forever, the company tries to show the benefit of what becoming an upgraded member can hold.
>
> ✓ *Vodafone*: Vodafone adopts a bundling business model. To lower the cost of attracting a single customer, the company attempts to bundle products to sell multiple goods to a single client (e.g. smartphone + internet plans). Bundling capitalises on existing customers by attempting to sell them different products. This can be incentivised by offering pricing discounts for buying multiple products.

Before thinking about growth, scalability, or even profitability, it is necessary to define, analyse, and assess a business model. Over the years, academics and practitioners have developed several models and frameworks [e.g. Chesbrough's (2006) business model template for open innovation, Mark Johnson's (2018) template for business model transformation, and the 10 dimensions of innovation defined by Keeley et al. (2013)], but only two frameworks have become viral among start-uppers and entrepreneurs: the Business Model Canvas and the Lean Canvas. These both are strategic tools used by entrepreneurs, start-ups, and managers to visualise and design their business models. These canvases help organisations clarify key aspects of their business and iterate on their strategies.

1.1.1. The Business Model Canvas

Developed by Alexander Osterwalder and Yves Pigneur (2010), the Business Model Canvas is a visual framework that consists of nine building blocks or components that together provide a comprehensive view of a business model. These building blocks are:

(1) *Customer segments*: Identifies the different groups of customers a business aims to serve.

(2) *Value proposition*: Describes the unique value that the business offers to each customer segment.

(3) *Channels*: Specifies the distribution and communication channels used to reach and engage with customers.

(4) *Customer relationships*: Defines the types of relationships established with customers (e.g. personal assistance, self-service, automated services).

(5) *Revenue streams*: Outlines how the business generates revenue from each customer segment.

(6) *Key resources*: Lists the essential assets, capabilities, and infrastructure required to deliver value.

(7) *Key activities*: Describes the core functions and activities necessary to operate the business.

(8) *Key partnerships*: Identifies external organisations or collaborators that play a vital role in the business model.

(9) *Cost structure*: Details the costs associated with running the business, including fixed and variable expenses.

The Business Model Canvas shown in Fig. 1 is a valuable tool for brainstorming, visualising, and analysing a business model. It encourages cross-functional collaboration and helps entrepreneurs and teams to quickly iterate and refine their business strategies.

Before defining growth strategies related to experiments, it can be useful to revisit the business model canvas to clarify the current business model, generate new ideas on products, services, channels, and other elements, and then define the experiments to be conducted and the hypotheses to be tested through data. Similarly, using growth hacking, as we will see, can be helpful for innovating the business model or making a pivot. The business model canvas can be used to clarify the new potential business model and discuss it with collaborators and consultants.

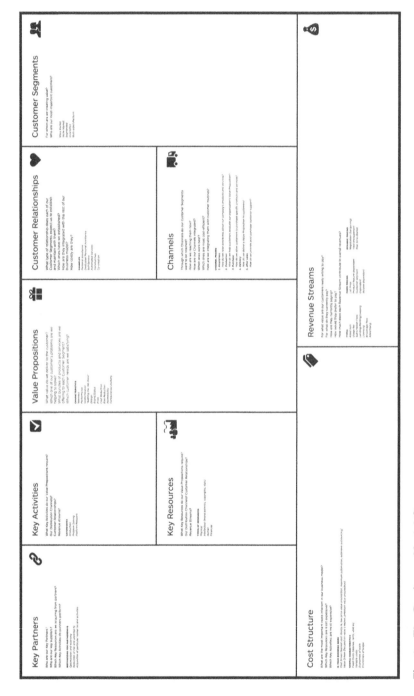

Fig. 1. The Business Model Canvas.
Source: Osterwalder et al. (2010).

1.1.2. Lean Canvas

The Lean Canvas, developed by Ash Maurya (2022), is a simplified version of the Business Model Canvas. It's particularly popular among start-ups looking for a quick and practical way to validate their business ideas. The Lean Canvas focusses on key aspects that are crucial for start-ups. The key building blocks of the Lean Canvas are:

- *Problem*: Identifies the top problems or needs that the start-up aims to address.
- *Solution*: Describes the unique solution or value proposition that the start-up offers to solve the identified problems.
- *Key metrics*: Specifies the key performance indicators that will be used to measure progress and success.
- *Unique value proposition*: Clearly articulates what makes the solution unique and why customers should choose it.
- *Unfair advantage*: Highlights any advantages, such as product's features, patents, expertise, or exclusive partnerships, that give the start-up an edge over competitors
- *Customer segments*: Identifies the specific customer segments that the start-up is targeting.
- *Channels*: Outlines the distribution and marketing channels the start-up will use to reach its customers.
- *Customer relationships*: Describes how the start-up plans to build and maintain relationships with customers.
- *Revenue streams*: Specifies the ways the start-up will generate revenue.
- *Cost structure*: Details the costs associated with running the start-up.

The Lean Canvas shown in Fig. 2 is designed for rapid experimentation and adaptation. It encourages entrepreneurs to focus on the most critical aspects of their business model and test their hypotheses quickly.

The Lean Canvas is more problem-centric, simplified, and geared towards start-ups looking to validate their ideas quickly. On the other hand, the Business Model Canvas offers a comprehensive view of the entire business model, making it suitable for a broader range of businesses, from start-ups to established companies, and emphasises the architecture of the business model as a whole. The choice between the two depends on the specific needs and objectives of the organisation or entrepreneur.

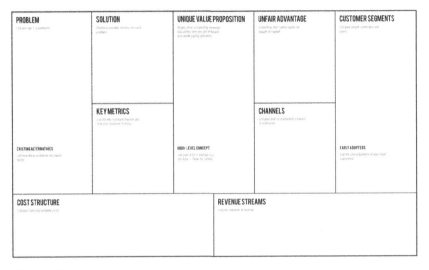

Fig. 2. The Lean Canvas.
Source: Maurya (2022).

Defining the business model before developing growth hacking strategies is important because it provides a strategic foundation for growth efforts. It helps ensure that growth initiatives are aligned with the organisation's objectives, target audience, revenue generation methods, resource allocation, and long-term sustainability. Understanding the business model is essential for effective competitive positioning and assessing scalability for rapid expansion.

As we will see in Chapter 4, the first key step in a growth strategy, according to Ryan Holiday, is to find the right product–market fit. In this sense, the Business Model Canvas and the Lean Canvas help to get clarity on what the company intends to offer in terms of products and services and the target audience problem it intends to solve. Another very useful tool for getting clarity on product–market fit, which is about the starting point of any business model, is the Value Proposition Canvas.

The Value Proposition Canvas (Osterwalder et al., 2015) is a strategic tool designed to help entrepreneurs and innovators better understand their customers' needs and to design products and services that directly address those needs. It operates on two main fronts: the Customer Profile and the Value Map.

The Customer Profile segment focusses on the customer's jobs-to-be-done, pains, and gains. 'Jobs' can be functional, social, or emotional tasks the customer is trying to accomplish. 'Pains' refer to anything that annoys the customers before, during, and after trying to get a job done. 'Gains' are the benefits or outcomes that customers hope to achieve.

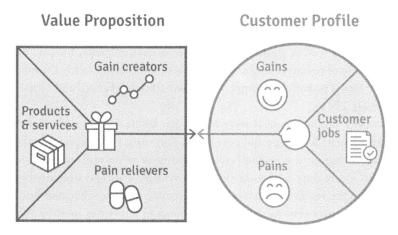

Fig. 3. The Value Proposition Canvas.
Source: Osterwalder et al. (2015).

On the other side, the Value Map details the products and services a business offers, the pain relievers that mitigate the customers' pains, and the gain creators that contribute to the customers' gains. This mapping ensures that the value proposition matches the customer's profile by addressing their core needs and alleviating their pains while enhancing their gains.

By using the Value Proposition Canvas, businesses can achieve a clearer understanding of what their customers truly value and how they can effectively meet these needs. This leads to the creation of products and services that are more likely to succeed in the market because they are designed with the customer's specific requirements in mind.

Employing the Value Proposition Canvas as shown in Fig. 3 allows for a structured approach to identifying and addressing customer pain points and gain points, thereby enhancing the overall value proposition. This tool is invaluable for start-ups and established businesses alike, as it facilitates a deeper connection with customers, ensuring that the solutions offered are not just innovative but genuinely valuable to the target audience.

1.2. BUSINESS MODEL DYNAMICS

As discussed, the concept of a business model has long been a foundational element in the fields of entrepreneurship, strategic management, and innovation. Traditionally, business models were perceived as static representations of how a firm creates, delivers, and captures value (Teece, 2010). However, in recent years, a profound shift has occurred within the academic discourse surrounding business models. This shift reflects the growing recognition that viewing business models as static dimensions may be insufficient to understand their role in contemporary business environments. Instead, an emerging body of research suggests that analysing business models through a dynamic lens is essential to comprehend their true significance and impact (Spieth et al., 2014).

Historically, business models were often regarded as fixed blueprints that outlined a company's strategy and operations. This static view emphasised the importance of crafting a sound and coherent business model upfront and then adhering to it over time. Such an approach provided clarity and structure but lacked the agility required to navigate the dynamic and ever-changing business landscape effectively. As the facts show, modern businesses must be able to adapt to market changes with agility, leveraging experiment-based methodologies such as growth hacking.

Following the need of companies, recent studies have introduced the concept of 'business model dynamics' (Foss & Saebi, 2018; Sanasi, 2023). These studies advocate for a dynamic perspective in viewing business models as adaptable and evolving constructs. This perspective acknowledges that the business environment is subject to continual change, driven by factors such as technological advancements, shifts in customer preferences, and competitive pressures.

The dynamic view of business models adopts a phenomenological stance, elevating the business model itself to the unit of analysis (Sanasi, 2023). This shift recognises the business model as a distinct and dynamic entity rather than a mere static representation of a firm's logic. Consequently, business model dynamics are seen as instrumental in understanding how companies navigate change and foster innovation.

One of the key implications of this dynamic perspective is its emphasis on the role of business models in fostering innovation. Within this context, the business model serves as a tool for managers and entrepreneurs to explore new markets and bring innovative products, ventures, and supporting networks into existence. It highlights how the adaptation and evolution of the business model itself can be a source of innovation. This is displayed in Fig. 4.

The dynamics of business models, thus, give the business model a performative function: the business model becomes the medium that embodies business opportunities and transmits them to stakeholders, serving as the interface between the business model and the stakeholders around it. As suggested by Sanasi (2023), business model dynamics fall into four categories: (1) business model validation, (2) business model scaling, (3) business model innovation, and (3) business model pivot.

Before to Begin

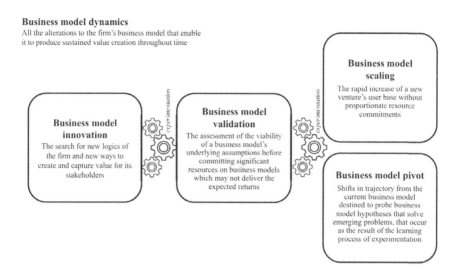

Fig. 4. Business Model Dynamics.
Source: Sanasi (2023). Used under Creative Commons Licence courtesy of Springer.

This framework offers a comprehensive lens to assess the evolutionary journey of a business over time. It recognises that all businesses, including those rooted in traditional sectors, are bound to evolve. Although the pace of evolution may vary, with traditional enterprises possibly moving at a slower rate, the imperative for change remains universal. Initially, a business must validate its business model, establishing a sustainable operation through effective mechanisms. Subsequently, it is essential to scale operations, expanding the business to the fullest potential defined by personal ambitions and the availability or accessibility of resources, including financial loans.

However, the business landscape is dynamic, often presenting significant shifts due to changes in the external environment. It is at these junctures that a business must consider innovating its business model or executing a strategic pivot to remain relevant and competitive.

Historically, several prominent companies have successfully navigated such transformations. For example, Netflix transitioned from a DVD rental service to a leader in streaming media and original content production, fundamentally altering its business model in response to technological advancements and changing consumer preferences. Similarly, Nokia, originally a paper mill company, pivoted through several industries including rubber and telecommunications before becoming a global giant in the mobile phone industry. These cases exemplify the critical importance of adaptability and strategic foresight in ensuring business longevity and success in a rapidly changing world.

1.2.1. Business Model Validation

Business model validation is a critical step in the entrepreneurial process, aimed at systematically testing and confirming the viability of a proposed business model. It goes beyond theoretical planning and involves gathering empirical evidence to ensure that the assumptions underlying the model are valid. This empirical validation is essential for reducing the inherent risks associated with new ventures. Validating a business idea means achieving what is known as problem-solution fit, that is, validating the solution at the centre of the business idea as the best possible solution to the problem of a particular customer segment, before launching it on the market. It therefore means making sure that potential customers perceive the problem to which our product or service is posed as a solution and are willing to pay to get it.

It is evident how the validation of a start-up idea is not an easy and immediate process: it consists of phases, tests, and analyses that lead from the collection of information about the customer to the study of the market, up to the development of a Minimum Viable Product that allows the actual product to be tested for the first time and in an exploratory way, gathering useful feedback for its improvement. The lean start-up approach, which will be covered in the next chapters, is a very effective method for validating a business model.

Dropbox is a notable example of business model validation. The company initially created a simple explainer video to demonstrate its cloud-based file storage and sharing service. The video quickly went viral, resulting in hundreds of thousands of sign-ups overnight. This real-world validation of user interest and demand laid the foundation for Dropbox's successful business model.

1.2.2. Business Model Scaling

Business model scaling involves expanding the reach and impact of a validated business model. It encompasses efforts to grow the organisation by replicating the existing model in new markets, segments, or geographic regions. Scaling often requires optimising operations, leveraging economies of scale, and developing strategies for sustainable growth. We are therefore at a later stage. The business model has been validated. The so-called product–market fit has been found. At this stage, then, the goal is to scale up to reach as many users as possible to cover fixed costs and start generating value. As we shall see, there are several useful tactics for scaling a business model efficiently and effectively.

1.2.3. Business Model Innovation

Business model innovation involves making significant changes to the core components of a company's business model to create new value propositions, revenue streams, or ways of delivering value. It is a strategic response to evolving market dynamics, technological advancements, and shifts in customer preferences.

For example, Apple's shift from a product-centric business model to a services-oriented ecosystem is a striking instance of business model innovation. The introduction of Apple Music, Apple Pay, and the App Store transformed the company's revenue streams. By expanding into services, Apple diversified its offerings and enhanced customer loyalty.

Innovating the business model therefore means altering one or more components of the business model. It is implemented when it is realised that the current business model does not create and/or capture value as before. For a movie-streaming platform, business model innovation may, for example, mean adding a formula that allows people to watch movies for free while 'tolerating' advertising.

1.2.4. Business Model Pivot

A business model pivot entails a fundamental change in a company's core business model components due to insights gained from market feedback or changing circumstances. It is a strategic manoeuvre often employed by start-ups when they encounter challenges or discover that their initial model is not gaining traction.

Slack initially started as a gaming company called Tiny Speck. When their game Glitch failed to gain traction, they pivoted their business model to develop a communication platform for teams. This pivot led to the creation of Slack, now a widely used tool for workplace collaboration.

> **Callout 2. The Evolution of the Business Model – Some Practical Examples**
>
> ✓ *Netflix*: Its original business model consisted in renting DVDs by mail. Netflix transitioned to a streaming service, offering a vast library of on-demand movies and TV shows. Netflix is now a global streaming giant, producing its own content and revolutionising the entertainment industry.

- ✓ *Amazon*: It was started as an online bookstore. It pivoted by expanding into an e-commerce platform, selling a wide range of products. Amazon is now one of the largest e-commerce and technology companies globally, offering services like Amazon Web Services (AWS), Kindle, and more.

- ✓ *3M*: This originally focussed on mining and manufacturing abrasives. The company evolved its business model into a diversified technology company, emphasising innovation and product diversification. 3M shifted its focus to developing a wide range of products, including adhesives, tapes, and various materials across different industries. 3M's pivot allowed the company to become a global leader in innovation, developing products in areas such as healthcare, transportation, and consumer goods.

- ✓ *Twitter (X)*: It was began as a podcasting platform called Odeo. Then it shifted focus to become a microblogging platform with the creation of Twitter. It has become a prominent social media platform with millions of active users worldwide.

2

DIGITAL BUSINESS MODELS

ABSTRACT

The concept of ecosystems has been integral to business strategy, evolving from general collaboration frameworks to innovation ecosystems driving technological progress. Digital ecosystems, initially rooted in engineering, now encompass manage-rial and strategic dimensions, are explored. Platforms, exemplified by companies like Amazon and Uber, epitomise this evolution, transitioning from linear value creation models to dynamic, multi-sided ecosystems leveraging external resources. These platforms, categorised as innovation or transaction platforms, harness network effects for exponential value creation. Effective platform management entails defining market sides, crafting unique value propositions, stimulating network effects, and solving the chicken-or-egg problem through strategic growth and engagement techniques. Governance mechanisms are crucial, encompassing value-sharing, leadership roles, and participation rules to sustain ecosystem growth. The chapter ponders the shift towards digital ecosystems and underscores the need for companies to adopt collaborative, flexible approaches, ensuring robust and sustainable business models in an increasingly interconnected and complex market environment.

Keywords: Digital business model; growth hacking; innovation; management; digital ecosystem; digital platform; platform management

2.1. AN INTRODUCTION TO DIGITAL ECOSYSTEMS

Ecosystem has frequently been associated with business strategy and activities (Peltoniemi & Vuori, 2004). Various terms have been used to define business ecosystems, including stakeholders collaborating to achieve specific goals (Moore, 1993) or stakeholders collaborating in general. Furthermore, there has been a growing interest in innovation ecosystems, where stakeholders collaborate to drive innovation (Adner & Kapoor, 2010), rather than solely focussing on improving existing businesses. This concept aligns with the principles of open innovation, which emphasise the acquisition of external knowledge by companies and the transfer of internal knowledge to external sources (Saura et al., 2022). Inbound and outbound open innovations, the mechanisms employed to facilitate these knowledge flows, are implemented to enhance performance, develop new products and processes, expedite time to market, and increase turnover (Santoro et al., 2020). This perspective supports prior research that suggests viewing an organisation not as a member of a single industry but as part of a business ecosystem spanning multiple industries. Consequently, it is reasonable to assert that the ecosystem concept does not seek to advocate for a paradigm shift in business management but rather recognises that companies exist within complex systems comprising diverse entities that evolve, mature, change, and adapt within dynamic environments. As a result, the concept of ecosystems has expanded over time, in line with the adoption of new business practices such as outsourcing, open innovation, participation in industrial clusters, and strategic alliances (Xie & Wang, 2020).

The term 'digital ecosystem' has recently emerged, initially with a strong engineering connotation, before evolving into a broader managerial and strategic perspective. Various definitions of digital ecosystems exist. Cusumano et al. (2019) recently proposed that 'Platforms, in general, connect individuals and organizations for a common purpose or to share a common resource', adding that they 'bring together individuals and organizations, enabling them to innovate or interact in ways that would otherwise be impossible, with the potential for nonlinear increases in utility and value'.

In summary, the rapid and continuous technological advancements have made it nearly impossible for companies to solely develop new products and services internally. Modern technological products rely on software and hardware integrations and modules that are difficult to develop and produce within a single company. This necessitates new open and participatory approaches and ecosystems, sometimes involving collaborations between competitors (Bresciani et al., 2018; Reischauer, 2024).

2.2. PLATFORMS AS DIGITAL ECOSYSTEMS

Over the past two decades, the emergence of digital companies operating on platform business models has been remarkable. Many of the successful companies today, commonly referred to as unicorns, are platforms (Cusumano et al., 2024). These platforms have made a significant impact across various industries and sectors. For example, in e-commerce, platforms like Amazon and Alibaba have revolutionised the way we buy and sell goods. In transportation, platforms such as Uber and Lyft have disrupted the traditional taxi industry. In finance, platforms like PayPal and Stripe have transformed online payments. In media, platforms like YouTube and Netflix have reshaped the consumption and creation of content.

These platforms, including Uber, Airbnb, Facebook, Amazon, Alibaba, Netflix, Apple, and Google, exemplify the ongoing shift from a linear and closed model of value creation ('pipeline') to an approach that leverages external resources for value generation (Nambisan et al., 2018). These resources are provided by a community of producers and consumers who often interchange their roles, as seen in the case of Airbnb guests and hosts or Uber drivers and passengers. Platforms serve as intermediaries, facilitating efficient connections between supply and demand through tools, algorithms, and rules.

Platforms have not only created new industries but also influenced and established new relationships and business models (Täuscher & Laudien, 2018). They can be considered powerful digital ecosystems characterised by complex and dynamic systems that involve multiple parties collaborating and sometimes competing to develop and mature the ecosystem itself. In response to factors like economic crises, globalisation, and uncertainty, platform-based business models have emerged rapidly, scaling up and disrupting traditional companies and incumbents. These models enable flexibility by leveraging external resources, aligning with the principles of open innovation (Hilbolling et al., 2020). For instance, Uber's business model relies on external resources such as cars and drivers, without which sustaining the model would be cost-prohibitive. The impact of platform companies can be seen in the decline of BlackBerry and Nokia due to competition from platform-based smartphones using Android and iOS, respectively. Blockbuster's failure is another well-known example attributed to competition from the Netflix platform.

In general, platforms connect individuals and organisations to pursue common purposes or share resources, enabling innovation and interactions that would otherwise be challenging, resulting in potential nonlinear growth in utility and value (Cusumano et al., 2019).

Platforms are complex systems characterised by intricate relationships, diverse dynamics, and mechanisms. Therefore, it is challenging to provide an exhaustive definition or explanation of all the mechanisms that govern them. Each platform is unique, with its own set of characteristics, strengths, and weaknesses. Additionally, the core elements and underlying business models of platforms often vary. Companies like Amazon have undergone significant changes over the years, while Alibaba took several years to find its winning formula. However, platforms can generally be classified into two broad types: innovation platforms and transaction platforms (Cusumano et al., 2019).

Innovation platforms serve as technological foundations on which other firms or individuals develop complementary innovations. The value of these platforms increases as the number and quality of complementary products and services grow, such as apps in the case of Android or video content for platforms like Netflix and Disney+. Often, these platforms experience indirect network effects, where the increasing availability of complementary offerings makes the platform more attractive to users, advertisers, investors, and other stakeholders. Examples of innovation platforms include Sony PlayStation, Apple iOS, Microsoft Windows, and Google Android. These platforms can be considered open innovation systems based on coupled processes.

On the other hand, transaction platforms function as intermediaries or online marketplaces where individuals and organisations can exchange or purchase data, information, products, and services. Direct network effects are especially significant for some of these platforms, as the perceived value by individual users increases with a larger user base. Examples of transaction platforms include Facebook, Twitter, Amazon Marketplace, Google Search, and WeChat.

From an economic and operational standpoint, platforms are known for their efficiency. Research conducted by Cusumano et al. (2019) revealed that platform-based companies outperform their counterparts in terms of market value, sales growth, and operating profits, all achieved with significantly fewer employees. These platforms leverage efficient business models based on the sharing economy's potential and open innovation strategies. The subsequent section will delve deeper into the platform business model, identifying its key management pillars.

2.3. BUSINESS MODELS OF PLATFORMS: FEATURES AND ISSUES

As previously mentioned, platforms are defined as systems that facilitate connections between individuals and organisations for a common purpose or resource sharing (Täuscher & Laudien, 2018). They enable innovation and interactions that would otherwise be difficult to achieve, leading to potential nonlinear increases in utility and value. This nonlinear growth occurs because each additional user gains access to the existing user base and innovations within the platform, resulting in exponential value creation for all participants (Parker & Van Alstyne, 2005). These network effects can extend across entire ecosystems, which encompass producers, suppliers, users, business partners, and other stakeholders, following an open innovation logic.

Given the complexity of platforms, effective management of resources and activities becomes crucial (Gawer, 2021). Not all platforms have successful business models, and not all of them can generate consistent profits. The key aspects of platform management are discussed in the following sections and summarised in Table 1.

Table 1. Platform Management Pillars.

#	Dimension	Implications for Business Model	Examples
1	Define the different sides of the market	Define specific VPs and who pays Define the main pillars of the business model	• Deliveroo has two main sides: riders and restaurants • Glovo has several sides including riders, restaurants, and retailers • WhatsApp has just one side (users). It exploits economies of scope, thanks to data, with other businesses (Facebook, Instagram) • Netflix's revenue model is based on a subscription model
2	Differentiate the business model	Better platform? Better service? Lower price? Better content? Communicate the uniqueness	• Amazon Prime Video offers a unique revenue model (a fee which gives access to many services) • Netflix has a strong focus on documentaries and exclusive content • Some platforms have a first mover advantage, which leads to quick adoption and high switching costs (WhatsApp)
3	Stimulate direct and indirect network effects	Try to stimulate network effects to increase the value of the platform	• WhatsApp: the value increases exponentially as the number of users increases – so it is better to give the service for free to users • Too good to go: indirect network effects – so it will be hard to get users without a high number of shops. So, how to stimulate adoption by shops?

(Continued)

Table 1. Platform Management Pillars. (*Continued*)

#	Dimension	Implications for Business Model	Examples
4	Solve the chicken-or-egg problem (in the case of multi-sided platforms)	Which side must bring onboard first? How?	
		1. Start small	1. Satispay, Tinder, and Facebook started small, on a geographical level. Same for Uber, setting up in a specific city to replicate and scale globally after
		2. Act as a producer	2. Google and Apple offer proprietary apps like mailing, calendar, etc.
		3. Bring onboard high-valued sides first	3. Streaming services use to bring onboard famous movies to attract users
		4. Platform Staging	4. It consists of evolving in two distinct steps: from a traditional vendor-based business model in the first stage to a platform-mediation business model in the second stage after reaching the critical user mass (Amazon)
		5. Subsiding	5. It typically consists of a subsidy side that allows the use of the platform with discounts or even for free, and a monetary side that is charged for participation or transactions. Uber gave free rides to users and convinced a few drivers to join the platform
		6. Platform Envelopment (partnering)	6. Spotify integrated into mobile operators' plans, Internet Explorer embedded in Microsoft OS
		7. Side switching	7. This involves making a two-sided platform one-sided by finding a platform design that allows users to fill both market sides of the MSP simultaneously (Airbnb where (with incentives) travellers can become hosts)
5	Explore opportunities for scope	New services? New stakeholders involved in the ecosystem?	Glovo allows to order groceries from supermarket. Ant financial offers insurance, loans, smart payments services, thanks to data acquired. Uber developed the UberEats service. Amazon with Fresh, Pharma, and Retail
6	Define governance mechanisms	Participation rules; value appropriation; incentives	iOS apps should meet certain standards; Uber drivers must have a driving license, meet the minimum age, at least one year of licensed driving experience in the US – or three years if you are under the age of 23, a valid US driver's license, use an eligible four-door vehicle

Source: Authors' elaboration.

2.3.1. Clearly Define the Various Sides of the Market

Platforms deliver products or services by bringing together two or more market sides that would not otherwise interact or easily connect. For example, Facebook connects users, advertisers, software developers, and companies looking for data, as well as content providers such as newspapers and magazines. Booking.com, a well-known travel fare aggregator and travel metasearch engine for lodging reservations, connects travellers with a wide range of accommodation options, enabling property owners to reach a global audience. Amazon marketplace connects sellers with buyers. Etsy, a marketplace for handmade goods, vintage items, and craft supplies, connects artisans and crafters with buyers looking for unique, handmade products. Satispay is a versatile mobile payment platform that connects a broad ecosystem, including users, shops, businesses, governments, and public administrations. By offering a simple, low-cost transaction system, it facilitates payments for goods, services, fines, and public fees, streamlining financial interactions across multiple sectors. This multi-sided platform exemplifies how digital innovation can enhance convenience and efficiency for all parties involved, driving widespread adoption, and transforming the traditional payment landscape.

It is crucial for the platform leader to understand the value that the platform offers to each side of the market. To achieve this, the platform leader should clearly define a specific unique selling proposition for each target segment. Furthermore, the leader should identify and leverage the resources, both tangible and intangible, brought by each participant to the ecosystem.

2.3.2. Define Your Own Unique Value Proposition and Business Model

It is vital to define the platform's unique value proposition and business model. One important aspect is determining which side of the platform pays, as this determines the economic sustainability of the business model. Many platforms do not charge users directly (e.g. WhatsApp, Facebook, X, Google, WeChat) but instead charge other sides such as advertisers, partners, or firms. Therefore, it is crucial to understand what companies are offering, specifically the value proposition, especially to those who will pay (e.g. data, advertising, contacts). Knowing which side of the market gets charged and which side gets subsidised is a critical business model decision for platforms. Additionally, it is necessary to ensure that the side that gets charged (e.g. users in the case of Uber) is large enough to cover both fixed and variable costs. For example, Spotify's business model requires a certain threshold of premium users to reach the break-even point. This shall guide strategies to convert a part of the target market from free users to premium users. Moreover, successful platforms may appear similar at first glance, and their business models may seem alike as well. However, successful platforms are built around unique value propositions and business models. For instance, Disney+ focusses on famous movies, while Netflix emphasises original series and documentaries. Amazon employs a unique revenue model, such as a subscription fee that provides access to various services like free delivery on the marketplace, space on the AWS cloud, and free digital books. The same differentiation applies to platforms like Telegram versus WhatsApp or Amazon versus eBay. Therefore, it is essential to identify aspects that make your company's digital business model unique. Finding niches in the market can often be advantageous.

2.3.3. Stimulate Direct and Indirect Network Effects, If Any

Many platforms experience the benefits of network effects, where the value of the platform exponentially increases as the number of users or organisations using it grows. Platforms like WhatsApp exhibit strong network effects, as the value of the platform increases exponentially with more users joining. The more users an individual knows on the platform, the more value they perceive from it. Similarly, platforms like Dropbox see their value increase as more users join because of the file-sharing capabilities. This type of network effect is known as 'direct' network effect.

In addition to direct network effects, platforms can also benefit from 'indirect' or 'cross-side' network effects. This occurs when one side of the market, such as users, attracts another side of the market, such as sellers or developers of complementary services. Platforms like Amazon or eBay exemplify this phenomenon. As the number of users on the platform increases, more sellers are incentivised to sell through the platform. To stimulate network effects, companies often employ growth hacking strategies (Bargoni et al., 2024), such as offering parts of a product or service for free or at a low cost to drive adoption and then monetising through other means. Discounts or incentives for users to bring their friends onto the platform are also common strategies. It's worth noting that network effects can create significant barriers to entry for new competitors. These barriers arise from the switching costs that the entire network of users would face if they were to switch to a new technology or platform. However, it's important to acknowledge that the creation of such barriers is becoming more challenging due to the increasingly fast and free movement of information and the adoption of open standards. Moreover, it's important to recognise that not all platforms experience positive network effects. Some platforms, like Uber, can face challenges when the number of users outweighs the number of drivers, leading to longer wait times per ride. Conversely, having an excess number of drivers compared to users can result in idle drivers and limited ride availability. Therefore, achieving a balance between the number of users and drivers in a given geographical area is crucial for such platforms. Overall, understanding and leveraging network effects are key considerations for platform leaders in building successful and sustainable platforms.

2.3.4. Solve the Chicken-or-Egg Problem

Customer acquisition is a core challenge for any born-digital company. Multi-sided platforms, namely those platforms having at least two sides in their business model (like Uber with users and drivers) can face the chicken or egg problem at an early-stage phase. It's not attractive for consumers to join the platform when there are no producers, and vice versa. This is called the chicken-and-egg problem. There are some ways through which this problem can be overcome, according to Cusumano et al. (2019), and Stummer et al. (2018).

(a) *Start small*: One approach is to start with a small structure and a limited customer base in a geographically restricted area. By focussing on a single city, region, or neighbourhood, companies can attract both suppliers and consumers more easily. This allows the company to prove the viability of the platform model to both sides and be more flexible in adapting and refining the model. Once successful, the platform can gradually expand, building the two sides in tandem, one area at a time. This strategy has been employed by car-sharing services like Uber or Lyft, as well as delivery services like Deliveroo, UberEats, and Glovo. The dating app Tinder, for example, was initially launched in specific colleges. To sum up, it consists of reducing the total market size and the required critical user mass. Fewer resources and less time are required to reach the critical inflexion point from which the multi-sided platform (MSP) can grow to other market segments (e.g. Uber setting up in a specific city to replicate and scale globally after).

(b) *Bring high-value users and partners on the platform first*: Another approach is to attract high-value users or partners to the platform first, using monetary incentives if necessary. By bringing on board members who contribute significant value, such as well-known movies for a movie streaming platform or popular products for an e-commerce platform, the platform can create a more enticing value proposition for the other side of the market. This strategy aims to leverage the presence of high-value participants to attract and convince other users or sides to adopt the platform.

(c) *Act as a producer*: In this strategy, the platform acts as a producer initially to attract an initial group of consumers. By offering products or services directly, the platform builds a user base. Once it has a solid consumer base, the platform can then leverage that user base to attract producers or suppliers to join the ecosystem. This strategy essentially starts as a traditional linear business and then evolves into a platform model as it scales. Google's Android platform is an example of this approach, as it initially developed key apps like Gmail and Calendar internally before opening up to external software developers to offer new apps. Similarly, Amazon initially fulfilled customer orders on its own but later opened up the Amazon Marketplace platform for third-party sellers.

(d) *Platform staging* (e.g. Amazon for bestseller books, OpenTable with a B2B value proposition). It consists of evolving in two distinct steps: from a traditional vendor-based (pipeline) business model in the first stage to a platform-mediation business model in the second stage after reaching the critical user mass.

(e) *Subsiding*: It typically consists of a subsidy side that allows the use of the platform with discounts or even for free, and a monetary side that is charged for participation or transactions.

(f) *Platform envelopment or ecosystem*: This partnering strategy relies on leveraging the shared relationships with (other) established platforms and their networks to strive to combine value propositions and benefit from a multiplatform bundle that leverages shared user relationships. (e.g. Spotify integrated into mobile operators' plans, Internet Explorer embedded in Microsoft OS).

(g) *Side switching*: This involves making a two-sided platform one-sided by finding a platform design that allows users to fill both market sides of the MSP simultaneously (e.g. eBay with collectors; Airbnb where (with incentives) travellers can become hosts).

These strategies help address the chicken-or-egg problem by gradually building both sides of the market or leveraging existing high-value participants to attract others. By carefully managing the initial growth and value proposition, platforms can overcome the challenge of attracting both sides and establish a thriving ecosystem.

Navigating the initial challenge of attracting both supply and demand, known as the 'chicken-or-egg' problem, can be daunting for start-ups launching multi-sided platforms. Orangogo, an innovative Italian platform designed to connect individuals with sports activities, exemplifies how to overcome this dilemma with strategic insight. We had the pleasure to interview the founder of Orangogo, who share her view on how they solved the chicken-or-egg problem and ignite growth.

From the outset, the awareness of the dilemma was acute. The platform needed sport clubs and associations to offer their courses to attract users, but simultaneously, users were needed to draw in more sport clubs and associations. The turning point came when Orangogo secured its first sport clubs and associations. This was pivotal not only in proving that the platform could indeed facilitate visibility and booking for sports courses but also in providing a tangible asset for search engine optimisation (SEO), thereby increasing the platform's online visibility.

SEO for the courses offered by the initial sport clubs and associations ensured that when people searched for sports activities online, Orangogo's platform – and the club's courses – appeared prominently. This visibility attracted the platform's first users. The successful registration and participation of these users validated the platform's effectiveness, encouraging the club or association to list more courses. It also played a crucial role in attracting more users and, subsequently, more sport clubs and associations.

The increased competition among clubs as the platform grew not only enriched Orangogo's offerings but also solidified its value proposition to both sides of the market. The importance of early strategic decisions, such as securing the first supplier and optimising for SEO, was key. It set off a chain reaction that helped build momentum. Attracting both sides of the market is an ongoing process, but initiating this movement is the most challenging part. Focussing on providing value and visibility for early adopters was the strategy that truly paid off for Orangogo.

Orangogo's story is a testament to the power of strategic thinking and leveraging early wins to overcome the daunting 'chicken-or-egg' problem faced by many platform start-ups. Through a combination of securing early adopters and leveraging digital marketing strategies like SEO, Orangogo has paved a path of growth, offering valuable lessons for emerging platforms navigating similar challenges.

2.3.5. Explore Opportunities for Scope

Network effects often drive economies of scale and scope in platform businesses. Amazon is a prime example of how expanding its offering and leveraging network effects has contributed to its success. Initially starting as an online bookstore, Amazon gradually expanded its product range to include various categories, which increased the platform's value proposition. This expansion attracted more vendors and users, leading to a positive feedback loop and further strengthening the network effects. In Amazon's case, economies of scope have become increasingly digital. The company has implemented a subscription-based business model, called Amazon Prime, where users pay an annual fee for benefits like fast shipping, access to video streaming services, and a vast library of books on Kindle. By offering a bundle of services and benefits, Amazon has been able to retain customers, create loyalty, and achieve economies of scale and scope. This approach enhances the overall value proposition for users and encourages them to stay within the Amazon ecosystem.

Moreover, diversification strategies have been observed in technology sectors among multinational companies like Amazon, Alibaba, Apple, and Google, as well as younger companies like Uber. These strategies involve the development of multiple ecosystems and the management of complexity across various business lines. By diversifying their offerings and expanding into new markets or industries, these companies aim to leverage their existing user base, brand recognition, and infrastructure to drive further growth and capture additional value. However, it's important to note that managing complexity and building and maintaining multiple ecosystems require significant resources, expertise, and strategic capabilities. Companies need to carefully balance their diversification efforts with effective resource allocation, operational efficiency, and the ability to maintain a coherent and consistent user experience across different offerings.

2.3.6. Define Precise Governance Mechanisms

The development of digital ecosystems is not easy, however. This requires strategy, vision, collaboration, shared values, and complementarity. According to Jacobides (2019), platforms' leaders should define various governance mechanisms focussing on the three following aspects.

(a) *Help members of the ecosystem in capturing value.* Successful ecosystems are those where value is shared, where many parts (not the ecosystem creators) succeed in capturing part of the value. This is because the ecosystem must offer not only a product but also complementary products and services. Those who develop/produce these complementary products and services must be able to capture part of the economic value to not leave the ecosystem. For example, Amazon Alexa and Google Nest represent hardware that exploits the Internet of

Things thanks to a series of complementary applications and software. Although not all of these applications will be successful, at least a part of them must capture value to strive in the market and allow the hardware to keep its usefulness. For the ecosystem, and especially for its leader, it will be important to offer incentives and motivation to the bulk of complementary developers.

(b) *Define the role played by the leader.* It is vital to define the role of the company that develops the ecosystem. Some leaders act as architects or orchestrators; sometimes, this role is entrusted to another player. Certainly, to be the leader, it is necessary to have a unique and difficult to imitate product or service (hardware or software). For example, Google is the leader of the ecosystem because it has a unique and non-replicable search engine. Apple is an ecosystem leader because it has a unique brand and design. This gives them a strong position in the ecosystem because developers will feel motivated to work with Apple and Google. The ecosystem leader should also be who is able, strategically, financially, and resource-wise, to change business models by adopting a risky entrepreneurial approach. In other terms, a company that can lead others to change.

(c) *Define precise participation rules.* To make the ecosystem flourish, it is important to define governance aspects. Some ecosystems are based on open systems, such as Uber, where drivers can be part of the ecosystem quickly and easily. On the other hand, in managed systems, access to the ecosystem is bound to some more restrictive criteria. For example, Apple developers must follow specific guidelines regarding pricing functionality. There are closed ecosystems where the criteria for access are very stringent. Finally, there are ecosystems where, to access, it is necessary to contractually bind oneself to guarantee the exclusivity of services for that ecosystem and not for others.

3

DEFINING GROWTH HACKING

ABSTRACT

This chapter explores the evolution and application of growth hacking (GH) as a methodology for rapidly scaling businesses. It begins by examining the initial wave of GH, characterised by unconventional tactics employed by digital firms like Dropbox, LinkedIn, and PayPal to achieve remarkable growth. These companies prioritise resource leveraging, outsourcing, and building rich ecosystems, capitalising on inherently scalable digital resources and network effects. The authors then delve into the concept of Customer Acquisition Cost (CAC) and its significance in evaluating business profitability and scalability, detailing its calculation and implications for strategic decision-making. Furthermore, they discuss the Customer Lifetime Value to Customer Acquisition Cost ratio (CLV/CAC ratio) as a key metric for assessing the efficiency and sustainability of customer acquisition strategies. Transitioning to the second wave of GH, the chapter explores debates surrounding its distinction from traditional digital marketing practices. Overall, the text provides a comprehensive overview of GH's past and present, highlighting its significance in driving business growth and innovation. Examining the dynamic landscape of digital marketing methodologies, while traditional digital marketing employs established tools and techniques within defined boundaries GH stands out for its experimental nature and systematic approach to innovation. This chapter draws on insights from industry experts and case studies.

Keywords: Growth hacking; customer acquisition cost; customer lifetime value; digital marketing; design thinking; evolution of growth hacking

3.1. FIRST WAVE: UNPRECEDENTED GROWTH THROUGH RESOURCE LEVERAGING

Growth hacking (GH), a concept conceived by Sean Ellis in the early 2010s, initially emerged as a creative means to rapidly 'hack' business growth. During its early stages, it often relied on unconventional methods and shortcuts to achieve rapid scaling.

Empirical evidence demonstrates that certain companies have harnessed their resources and capabilities in an extraordinary manner, resulting in unprecedented growth. Prominent examples include companies such as Dropbox, LinkedIn, Pinterest, and PayPal, among others. These companies, often referred to as digital firms or digital platforms (Cusumano et al., 2019), distinguish themselves from traditional industrial firms by adopting business models that prioritise the non-integration of resources and activities, relying extensively on outsourcing and building rich ecosystems.

Taking a resource-based view perspective (Sedera et al., 2016), these digital firms harness digital resources that are inherently scalable, owing in part to network effects.[1] This begs the question: How did these companies effectively manage their resources and activities to attain such remarkable growth, and what made their business models highly scalable?

A common thread that unites these successful companies is their adept utilisation of GH to facilitate rapid expansion. For instance, PayPal employed a groundbreaking hack by incentivising individuals to sign up. The company recognised that the lifetime value (LTV) of newly acquired customers exceeded the cost of offering a $10 reward each time a referred friend created an account. Similarly, Airbnb devised a simple yet impactful strategy to significantly boost their booking numbers: enhancing the quality of property photos listed on their platform. To enhance image quality, Airbnb initially dispatched their teams to personally photograph hosts' apartments. Subsequently, they scaled this approach by hiring a network of photographers worldwide to meet the demand. Furthermore, Airbnb ingeniously leveraged the Craigslist API through reverse engineering. This innovation allowed Airbnb users to effortlessly cross-post their property listings on Craigslist, tapping into an extensive user base that already existed.

Callout 3. Customer Acquisition Cost

Customer Acquisition Cost (CAC) is a key metric in business, especially for platforms, which refers to the total cost of acquiring a new customer. In the context of platforms – which could be digital marketplaces, social media platforms, software as a service (SaaS) product, or any other online service that connects different user groups – CAC plays a crucial role in understanding the business's profitability and scalability.

For Platforms, Calculating CAC Typically Involves Several Components:

- *Marketing and advertising expenses*: This includes all the costs associated with marketing and advertising efforts aimed at attracting new users to the platform. These can range from digital marketing campaigns (like Google Ads, Facebook Ads) to traditional marketing methods (like TV commercials, print ads).

- *Sales and promotion costs*: This includes expenses related to sales teams, promotional offers, discounts, or any other sales activities used to attract new customers. For instance, a platform might offer a free trial or a discount on the first purchase to entice sign-ups.

- *Technology and infrastructure costs*: For digital platforms, a portion of the technology and infrastructure costs (like hosting services, data analytics tools, customer support software) is often attributed to acquiring new customers.

- *Personnel costs*: This includes salaries and commissions for staff involved in marketing, sales, and customer support roles, as they play a role in acquiring and onboarding new customers.

To calculate CAC for a platform, it is necessary to sum up all these costs over a specific period and then divide them by the number of new customers acquired during that period.

$$CAC = Total\ Costs\ Associated\ with\ Customer\ Acquisition / Number\ of\ New\ Customers\ Acquired$$

Understanding CAC is essential for platforms because it helps in evaluating the effectiveness of marketing strategies and in making informed decisions about resource allocation. A high CAC might indicate that the platform is spending too much to acquire each customer, which can be unsustainable in the long run, especially if the LTV of a customer is not significantly higher than the CAC. Conversely, a low CAC suggests efficient use of resources in attracting customers.

Moreover, in platform businesses where network effects are crucial, balancing the acquisition of different types of users (like buyers and sellers in a marketplace, or service providers and consumers in a service platform) is vital. The CAC needs to be optimised for each user group to ensure sustainable growth and profitability.

Example – CAC Calculation

Let's Consider a Subscription-Based Business, Such as a Saas Company, Which Incurs Various Costs in Acquiring New Customers:

- *Digital marketing expenses*: The company spends $50,000 on digital marketing efforts, including online advertising, content marketing, and social media campaigns over a specific period.

- *Sales team costs*: The company has a dedicated sales team responsible for converting leads into customers. The total cost of the sales team, including salaries, commissions, and associated expenses, is $30,000 during the same period.

Let's imagine that through these marketing and sales efforts, the company successfully acquires 1,000 new customers.

Now, let's calculate the CAC:

CAC=Total Marketing and Sales Expenses/Number of New Customers Acquired

CAC=$50,000+$30,000/1,000

CAC=$80,000/1,000

CAC=$80

In this hypothetical example, the CAC is $80 per new customer. This means that, on average, the company spent $80 in marketing and sales expenses to acquire each of the 1,000 new customers during the specified period. It's important for the company to analyse this cost in relation to the LTV of a customer and overall business profitability.

The Customer Lifetime Value to Customer Acquisition Cost ratio (CLV/CAC ratio)

The return on customer acquisition investment is a key metric used to evaluate the efficiency and sustainability of a company's customer acquisition strategy. This ratio compares the value a company expects to derive from a customer over their lifetime to the cost of acquiring that customer.

The formula for CLV/CAC ratio is:

$$CLV/CAC\ Ratio = Customer\ Lifetime\ Value\ (CLV)/Customer\ Acquisition\ Cost\ (CAC)$$

where:

- CLV represents the total revenue a company expects to earn from a customer throughout their entire relationship. It considers factors such as the customer's average purchase value, frequency of purchases, and the expected duration of the customer relationship.
- CAC is the cost associated with acquiring a new customer. It includes expenses related to marketing, advertising, and sales efforts.

The CLV/CAC ratio provides insights into the overall health of a business's customer acquisition and retention strategy. A ratio above 1 typically indicates a healthy and sustainable business model. A ratio below 1 may suggest that the cost of acquiring customers is too high relative to the value those customers bring over their lifetime.

An Example

If CLV is $800 and CAC is $200, the CLV/CAC ratio would be 800/200=4.

This means that, on average, the company expects to earn four times the amount it invested in acquiring each customer.

Companies aim to maintain a CLV/CAC ratio that ensures profitability and sustainability. A ratio that is too low may indicate the need to optimise marketing and sales processes or focus on increasing customer retention to improve the overall financial health of the business.

CAC as Driver for Growth Strategies

CAC is a Crucial Metric That Helps Managers in Guiding Several Company's Growth Strategies, as an Example:

- *Resource allocation and budgeting*: Businesses can better allocate their marketing and sales budgets. A high CAC might indicate the need to invest in more efficient marketing channels or sales strategies, whereas a low CAC suggests an opportunity to scale efforts in successful areas to boost growth.

- *Profitability and pricing strategy*: If the cost to acquire a customer is too high relative to the customer's LTV, the business model may not be sustainable. Companies might adjust their pricing strategies or work to increase the LTV to ensure a healthy LTV:CAC ratio, which is critical for long-term growth.

- *Target market focus*: Understanding CAC for different segments can drive strategic decisions regarding target markets. If certain segments have a significantly lower CAC, companies might focus their growth strategies on these markets.

- *Product and service development*: Insights from CAC calculations can influence product development. For instance, if acquiring customers for a specific product is too costly, a company might invest in modifying the product, enhancing its value proposition, or developing new products that meet market needs more effectively.

- *Market entry and expansion decisions*: CAC plays a vital role in decisions about entering new markets or expanding within current ones. A low CAC in a new market could indicate a growth opportunity, while a high CAC could suggest that entering a market might not be cost-effective.

- *Investment and funding*: Investors often look at CAC and the LTV/CAC ratio to assess a company's efficiency and scalability. A favourable ratio can attract investment, which can be used to fuel growth. Conversely, a high CAC may require strategic changes to make the business more attractive to investors.

In summary, CAC is not just a measure of marketing and sales efficiency; it's a comprehensive metric that influences strategic decisions across the entire business. Optimising CAC can lead to more efficient growth, better resource allocation, and improved profitability, all of which are crucial for a company's success and expansion.

To sum up, GH has been conceived as a methodology to acquire users and scale a start-up after the launch phase. It is related to what has been called as Traction by Gabriel Weinberg, the founder of DuckDuckGo, and Justin Mares (2015) in their book *Traction: How Any Startup Can Achieve*

Explosive Customer Growth. The book is particularly popular among entrepreneurs and start-up enthusiasts. The central thesis of the book is that start-ups often fail not because of product problems but because they don't get enough traction. Traction, in this context, refers to the ability of a company to attract and retain customers. Weinberg and Mares outline a framework for achieving this traction, detailing various channels and strategies that start-ups can use to acquire customers.

One of the key concepts in the book is the Bullseye Framework, which is a method for determining the most effective marketing channels to focus on. This framework involves three steps: brainstorming every possible traction channel, testing channels quickly and cheaply to determine which have potential, and then focussing on the channels that work best to maximise traction.

The book covers 19 different channels that start-ups can use to gain traction:

(1) *Viral marketing*: Using existing social networks to spread product information and drive brand awareness.

(2) *Public relations (PR)*: Reaching audiences through media coverage and press releases.

(3) *Unconventional PR*: Doing something exceptional or outrageous to attract media attention.

(4) *Search engine marketing (SEM)*: Using paid advertising on search engines to reach potential customers.

(5) *Social and display ads*: Using ads on social media platforms and other websites.

(6) *Offline ads*: Traditional advertising methods such as TV, radio, billboards, newspapers, and magazines.

(7) *Search engine optimisation (SEO)*: Optimising website content to rank higher in search engine results for relevant keywords.

(8) *Content marketing*: Creating and distributing valuable, relevant content to attract and engage a target audience.

(9) *Email marketing*: Using email to communicate with and market to potential and existing customers.

(10) *Engineering as marketing*: Using engineering resources to create tools and resources that reach more customers.

(11) *Targeting blogs*: Getting coverage or placing guest posts on relevant blogs.

(12) *Business development (BD)*: Creating strategic partnerships that provide leverage for growth.

(13) *Sales*: Directly selling to the customer through various sales models.

(14) *Affiliate programmes*: Partnering with other businesses or individuals who promote your product in exchange for a commission.

(15) *Existing platforms*: Leveraging existing platforms (like the App Store, Amazon, or major social networks) to reach more customers.

(16) *Trade shows*: Participating in trade shows to meet with potential customers, partners, and influencers in your industry.

(17) *Offline events*: Hosting or attending events such as meetups, conferences, or workshops.

(18) *Speaking engagements*: Speaking at events to build authority and gain exposure.

(19) *Community building*: Building a community around your brand or product to foster customer loyalty and word-of-mouth.

Each of these channels offers different advantages and can be suitable for different types of businesses and stages of growth. The key is to test and evaluate which channels work best for the company's specific business context.

The 19 channels of customer acquisition detailed in the book are applicable not just to start-ups and platforms but to virtually any type of business. These channels are broadly relevant and can be adapted to different industries, business models, and company sizes. The key is to understand how each channel can be leveraged in the context of a specific business's goals, target audience, and resources.

Overall, it is a highly versatile model, as each channel has a wide range of applications. For example, content marketing can be used by a small local business or a large multinational corporation. Moreover, it is highly scalable and adaptable, as channels like SEO or social media marketing can be scaled according to the resources available. A small business might start with a modest budget and grow its efforts as it expands. In a similar way, different channels can be adapted to suit different markets and customer segments. For example, email marketing can be tailored to both B2B and B2C audiences.

These are just examples of how a company can experiment with different marketing channels to scale. In experimentation, creativity plays a fundamental role. Marketers use creativity to generate innovative ideas for scaling a business model exponentially.

There are many other examples of companies which grew a lot in the past thanks to GH strategies, as Callout 4 shows.

Callout 4. Example of Growth Hacking Strategies

- *Dropbox – Referral programme*: Dropbox's referral programme is one of the most famous GH success stories. They offered existing users additional storage space for free if they referred new users to the platform. This simple incentive-driven referral programme helped Dropbox grow from 100,000 users to over 4 million in just 15 months.

- *LinkedIn – Email importer*: LinkedIn's 'import your email contacts' feature encouraged users to connect with their email contacts already on the platform. This strategy not only expanded LinkedIn's user base but also facilitated connections between users, enhancing engagement.

- *Uber – Free rides for referrals*: Uber used a referral programme that rewarded both the referrer and the referee with free rides. This incentivised existing users to refer new riders and drivers, driving user acquisition and growth in new markets.

- *Hotmail – Viral email signature*: Hotmail famously included a default email signature at the end of every sent email, inviting recipients to sign up for a free Hotmail account. This viral marketing tactic helped Hotmail acquire millions of users rapidly.

- *Instagram* – Cross-promotion: Instagram strategically cross-promoted its platform on other social media networks like Facebook and Twitter. This helped them attract users from these platforms to Instagram, leading to rapid user growth.

- *Tinder – Gamified swiping*: Tinder gamified the dating experience with its swiping feature. Users could quickly swipe right or left to indicate interest in potential matches, making the app engaging and addictive, which contributed to its growth.

- *PayPal – Monetary incentives*: In its early days, PayPal offered $10 to new users and $10 to those who referred them. This not only encouraged sign-ups but also created a strong network effect as more people adopted the service.

- *HubSpot – Content marketing*: HubSpot used content marketing to attract users. They created valuable blog posts, ebooks, and webinars that answered common marketing and sales questions. This content not only drove organic traffic but also positioned HubSpot as an authority in its industry.

- *Zynga – Social Sharing in Games*: Zynga, the developer behind popular games like FarmVille, encouraged players to share their in-game achievements and invitations with friends on social media. This viral loop helped Zynga games spread quickly on platforms like Facebook.

3.2. SECOND WAVE: FROM GH TO GROWTH

As discussed, it is possible to assert that GH had an initial wave, during which it was considered an approach to scale a business model rapidly and efficiently. This aligns with the definition provided by Sean Ellis. He defined GH as 'a process of rapid experimentation across the full customer journey to accelerate customer and revenue growth'.

From this viewpoint, GH is often seen as a strategy that utilises elements of digital marketing to accelerate business growth through users' acquisition. It involves employing creative and unconventional tactics within the digital landscape. However, it's worth noting that there has been criticism and debate regarding whether GH is truly distinct from traditional digital marketing practices.

Some critics argue that GH is merely a repackaging of existing digital marketing techniques, such as email marketing, social media campaigns, SEO, SEM, and other well-established methods, including the one suggested by Weinberg and Mares. Some contend that GH doesn't introduce fundamentally new concepts but rather combines these existing techniques in innovative ways.

For example, consider Airbnb's growth strategy mentioned earlier. While it involved leveraging Craigslist and other digital channels, one could argue that it incorporated elements of traditional online marketing, such as partnerships and cross-promotion. The debate lies in whether the unique combination of these techniques, the timing, and the creative execution make GH substantially different from traditional digital marketing.

In essence, according to some scholars and practitioners, GH can be viewed as an evolution or adaptation of digital marketing, where the focus is on rapid experimentation, data-driven decision-making, and unconventional approaches to achieve growth objectives.

The distinction may not always be clear-cut, as successful GH often blurs the line between marketing, product development, and user experience optimisation.

However, this isn't entirely accurate. Digital marketing indeed utilises specific tools to boost sales, enhance brand awareness, and achieve various marketing goals. On the other hand, GH is a working methodology rooted in experimentation and data-driven decision-making, akin to a scientific approach to innovation. What sets GH apart is its versatility – it can be applied to various domains beyond just sales and marketing.

Callout 5. An Interview with Raffaele Gaito, Growth Hacking Expert

- The existence of multiple definitions does raise some concerns for me regarding the concept of GH. It is quite evident what GH entails, especially when we consider Sean Ellis, the founding figure of this methodology, who initiated it nearly 11 years ago. He recently revisited this topic with a rather assertive post on LinkedIn, perhaps a few months ago, where he expressed his frustration with the excessive diversification of definitions, the constant association with gimmicks, hacks, and subterfuge. In essence, GH is simply an experimentation process.

- In my view, there is little room for ambiguity in understanding GH. It is a methodology that empowers companies to experiment methodically. Much of what is portrayed as part of the larger narrative surrounding American case studies can be attributed to the pop culture of GH. Those who seek to garner easy likes on LinkedIn readily reference examples like Dropbox, attracting a flurry of likes.

- Methodologically speaking, GH is a precisely defined concept. It offers a structured approach for companies to experiment. Innovation within companies is achieved through experimentation, and when faced with the need to experiment, there are two ways to proceed. You can either go about it in a disorganised, crude, or in-house manner, sporadically remembering to experiment, or you can experiment systematically. This is where GH comes into play.

> It involves working with data, employing the appropriate reference frameworks, following a predefined process, and involving specific roles within the company, along with distinct phases, and so on.
>
> - It is akin to defining what agile or lean methodologies are. They are universal methods defined once in literature, and they will forever remain the same. Over the years, their applications might evolve, along with the supporting tools, but the core methodology remains intact. To put it more explicitly, in my opinion, GH is the scientific method applied within a company. It involves conducting experiments, validating hypotheses in a controlled environment, analysing data, and having the ability to replicate these experiments. If successful replication occurs, it's deemed acceptable; otherwise, the approach is discarded, and one continues onward.

Digital marketing predominantly relies on established tools and techniques tailored to specific marketing objectives. It encompasses strategies such as content marketing, email campaigns, SEO, PPC advertising, and social media management, each designed to achieve specific marketing outcomes. While effective, these approaches often operate within predefined boundaries and established norms.

Conversely, GH is characterised by its experimental nature, like the interview with Raffaele Gaito underlined (Callout 5). It involves continuously testing novel ideas, strategies, and tactics, driven by data analysis and iterative learning. The key distinction lies in its systematic approach to innovation. GH extends beyond traditional marketing functions and can be applied to product development, user experience enhancement, customer retention strategies, human resource management, and more. Recently it has also been proposed as a methodology to innovate business models (Sanasi, 2023).

In essence, while digital marketing leverages established tools and practices to achieve marketing goals, GH is a dynamic and experimental approach that transcends marketing boundaries, making it a valuable methodology for innovation across various business domains. In other words, it can be asserted that digital marketing serves GH. Marketing provides the tools to implement the growth methodology, which relies on continuous experimentation.

The distinctiveness of GH lies in its utilisation of (big) data to instil a data-driven decision-making culture within the company. It also employs an iterative approach to address innovation or swiftly prototype designs, enabling the interception of customer needs throughout the customer journey

(Bohnsack & Liesner, 2019). These elements of GH harness the power of big data analysis and continuous learning through iterative experimentation. This enables companies to adapt their capabilities to the ever-evolving competitive landscape. Big data analytics encompass a complex set of tools and analytical techniques used to store, manage, analyse, and visualise vast and intricate datasets (Troisi et al., 2020). These tools and techniques increasingly bolster decision-making processes within firms. In this context, GH asserts that companies should transform data into actionable information, which can then be translated into knowledge to foster learning and creativity. This forms a cyclical process of continuous improvement. Practically, GH is the process of rapidly experimenting with and implementing resource-light and cost-effective tactics to acquire and retain an active user base, sell products, and efficiently scale the business. It relies on traceable marketing tools, allowing data from specific stages of the customer journey or funnel to be analysed to make informed decisions and test hypotheses.

From the foregoing discussion, it is evident that the literature has predominantly treated GH as a process rooted in marketing strategies, primarily effective in the digital firm context.

However, following the discussion so far, it is possible to infer that GH witnessed two phases.

The first phase viewed it as a series of marketing activities aimed at rapidly scaling a business (as per Sean Ellis' vision). The second phase, currently unfolding since the pandemic, positions GH as a methodology for testing and enhancing processes, activities, products, services, and business models through data-driven experiments. Hence, over time, the concept of GH has evolved into a comprehensive and systematic approach that focusses on several pillars:

(1) *Experimentation:* GH is grounded in a culture of experimentation. It revolves around constantly testing new ideas, strategies, and tactics across the entire customer journey. This process involves A/B testing, multivariate testing, and other data-driven experiments to refine and optimise approaches. For example, let's imagine a fitness company wanting to increase user engagement and retention for a fitness tracking app. A possible experiment is to implement a push notification optimisation test. The working hypothesis could be that sending personalised push notifications at different times of the day will increase user engagement and retention. The design of the experiment involves a variable (i.e. timing of push notifications) and three groups of users. Group A, users that receive push notifications in the morning, and Group B, users that receive push notifications in the evening,

and a control Group, a subset of users that do not receive any push notifications. As measurement metrics we can use User Engagement (number of times users open the app) and Retention Rate (percentage of users who continue using the app after a week). Group A and Group B users receive personalised push notifications based on their historical app usage patterns. The control group continues to use the app without any additional push notifications. The experiment consists in monitoring user engagement and retention metrics for a set period (e.g. two weeks) and compare the results between the groups to determine if there's a significant difference. If Group A or Group B shows a significant improvement in engagement and retention compared to the control group, the optimised timing can be implemented for all users. If there's no significant difference or negative impact, further experiments with different variables (e.g. message content, frequency) can be conducted. Based on the results, further experiments can be designed to refine the push notification strategy continually. For example, if timing is found to be crucial, subsequent experiments may focus on refining the time window further. By conducting experiments like this, growth hackers can identify strategies that resonate with users, leading to improved user engagement and long-term retention for the fitness tracking app.

(2) *Data-driven decision-making:* Central to GH is the reliance on data and analytics. It prioritises making decisions based on empirical evidence and employs data to guide strategies and campaigns. This data-driven approach enables growth hackers to uncover valuable insights, refine their approaches, and maximise results. For example, imagine an e-commerce platform that wants to increase the conversion rate (CR) on its product pages. The company will have to monitor the CR on product pages with the help of analytics tools to collect data on user interactions with the product pages and to track metrics such as page views, click-through rates, and actual purchases. If, for example, providing clearer product descriptions and improving the visibility of the 'Add to Cart' button will positively impact the CR, the company could implement an A/B test on a sample of product pages to monitor and collect data on user interactions with both variants over a defined period. If one variant shows a significant increase in the CR and a decrease in bounce rates, it suggests that the modifications are positively influencing user behaviour. Continuously monitor the impact of the changes on the overall CR and using real-time data to identify any unexpected trends or issues the e-commerce platform can make informed changes to its product pages, leading to increased CRs and improved overall user experience.

The iteration process in GH involves a continuous cycle of testing, learning from the results, and making data-driven adjustments to improve the effectiveness of growth strategies.

(3) *Trial and error:* GH acknowledges that not all experiments will succeed. It embraces a trial-and-error mindset, where failures are viewed as opportunities to learn and iterate. By continuously testing and iterating, growth hackers uncover strategies that yield the best results. In other words, in the growth methodology, failure is accepted because it helps to understand what 'doesn't work' in order to eventually determine what 'works'. This aspect aligns with the earlier assumptions that GH is based on continuous experiments to test hypotheses.

(4) *Cross-functional collaboration:* GH is a collaborative endeavour that often involves teams from various departments, including marketing, product development, engineering, and more. It fosters a culture of breaking down silos to create a cohesive strategy focussed on driving growth. The effectiveness of GH strategies is usually contingent on the presence of a well-rounded team equipped with a diverse range of cross-functional skills, encompassing marketing, product development, programming, finance, leadership, and more. For example, a tech start-up that aims to increase user engagement and retention for its mobile app, which provides a platform for freelance professionals to connect with clients seeking specific services, needs the cross-collaboration of two teams: the content and product teams. The content team is responsible for creating blog posts, infographics, and educational content related to freelance work, career tips, and industry trends, while the product team manages the development and user experience of the mobile app. The two teams work together to plan an integrated campaign that includes the release of new app features along with the rollout of complementary content.

(5) *User-centric approach:* A fundamental tenet of GH is an unwavering focus on the user or customer. It involves understanding user behaviour, identifying pain points, and catering to their needs. This knowledge shapes strategies and experiences that resonate with the target audience. From this perspective, GH works well as an approach to constantly improving the value proposition. Frequently, experiments revolve around consumer behaviour and preferences, which guide the choices and adaptations needed.

(6) *Scalability and sustainability:* While GH may have originated as a quick hack, it has evolved to prioritise scalable and sustainable growth. The goal

is not just to acquire users or customers but to retain and nurture them for long-term success. In other words, as we will see, GH works well for scaling but also for optimisation, including retention, and improvement.

(7) *Virality and referral programmes:* Encouraging users to refer others and share products or content is a key GH tactic. Viral loops and referral programmes are often used to stimulate organic growth through word-of-mouth and social sharing. However, the effectiveness of virality strategies largely depends on the industry type and business model, primarily linked to the presence of network effects. Virality works well when users have monetary and non-monetary incentives for recommending the product or service. In the case of non-monetary incentives, users might recommend the product or service because they feel deeply engaged with the value proposition, which leads to organic word-of-mouth.

(8) *Product–market fit:* Ensuring that a product or service aligns perfectly with the needs of a target market is essential. Growth hackers work to identify and refine this fit to drive user adoption and satisfaction. As we will see, ensuring a product–market fit is more related to the lean start-up methodology. Despite this, GH can be implemented to steadily innovate the product to ensure market attractiveness and retention. This requires a continuous effort in analysing the consumer to identify critical points and improve the product continually. A/B tests are conducted precisely for this purpose.

(9) *Automation and tools:* Automation and specialised GH tools are leveraged to streamline processes, save time, and increase efficiency. These tools can help with tasks like email marketing, lead generation, and analytics. Automation can be applied to many processes and activities within an organisation. For example, a company might use a website or a landing page with a sign-up form to capture leads. This form could offer something of value in exchange for the visitor's email address, like a free e-book, a webinar registration, or a discount code. Once the email is captured, the lead is entered into an automated email marketing sequence. This sequence is pre-designed and consists of a series of emails that are sent out at pre-determined intervals. The email sequence is designed to engage and nurture the leads. Early emails might provide valuable information related to the lead's interests. Subsequent emails might showcase success stories, customer testimonials, or further incentives (like additional discounts or exclusive content).

(10) *Creativity and innovation:* Growth hackers often think outside the box and come up with creative, unconventional solutions to growth

challenges. Innovation is a driving force behind successful GH. Digital tools support the growth patterns. However, creative thinking still matters a lot. Creativity is employed to generate ideas for testing. As we will see later, GH can be implemented by following the phases of goal definition or problem identification, idea generation, prioritisation, and execution. In the phase related to idea generation, creativity and brainstorming are key.

(11) *Customer retention:* While acquisition is important, retaining existing customers is equally crucial. GH strategies have expanded to include customer retention efforts, such as loyalty programmes and personalised experiences. The Duolingo case discussed in the following exhibit precisely addresses the importance of retention.

(12) *Continuous learning:* Growth hackers are constantly learning and adapting. They stay up-to-date with industry trends, emerging technologies, and evolving consumer behaviour to remain effective.

(13) *Agility:* Flexibility and agility are vital in the fast-paced world of GH. Being able to pivot quickly in response to data and feedback is a key characteristic of successful growth hackers.

Callout 6. Case Study: Duolingo's User Retention Strategy

Introduction: Duolingo, the popular language learning app, faced a critical decision point in its growth journey. Recognising the need to shift its focus from lead generation to user retention, the company adopted a data-driven approach to reshape its strategy.

Challenge: Duolingo initially prioritised lead generation to attract new users. However, it realised that long-term success depended on keeping users engaged over time. To address this challenge, Duolingo decided to segment the targets, distinguishing among daily active users (DAUs), weekly active users (WAUs), and monthly active users (MAUs).

Strategy:

1. *Metric innovation:* Duolingo introduced new metrics, focussing on DAUs, WAUs, and MAUs to measure user engagement comprehensively. These metrics provided valuable insights into different user segments, highlighting the importance of daily interaction.

2. *Retention over acquisition*: Through statistical analysis, Duolingo's growth team discovered that users who engaged daily demonstrated higher long-term value. They were more likely to stay with the platform, thus increasing the CLV. Since Duolingo offers language learning services, users have a better chance of learning if they enter the platform every day. This should make him/her more satisfied and more likely to recommend the app to friends and family.

Execution: Duolingo invested in user experience enhancements, such as gamification elements, personalised learning paths, and daily challenges. These features encouraged daily usage and maintained user interest over time.

Results: By shifting its focus towards user retention and leveraging the new engagement metrics, Duolingo witnessed significant improvements:

- A steady increase in DAUs, indicating enhanced user engagement.
- Improved user satisfaction and loyalty, resulting in longer customer lifetimes.
- Enhanced profitability as retained users contributed more to the company's bottom line.

Conclusion: Duolingo's strategic shift from lead generation to user retention, supported by innovative metrics and a commitment to daily user engagement, transformed the company's growth trajectory. By recognising the value of retained users and investing in their experience, Duolingo not only improved its user base but also its long-term profitability.

In conclusion, the case demonstrates that GH is not always employed solely for customer acquisition and scaling. It is often used to conduct experiments to understand the most effective growth path.

These pillars collectively form the foundation of GH strategies, guiding practitioners as they seek to achieve rapid and sustainable growth for their businesses or projects.

Successful adaptation to changes necessitates structured processes, systems, and a focus on forecasting trends, monitoring the competitive landscape, and understanding the drivers of change. Organisational development plays a pivotal role in sustaining strategy, fostering an innovative culture, and embracing new customers, markets, and technologies.

In this context, GH emerges as a powerful approach for systematically and organised change. It's important to dispel the notion that GH is solely for high-tech or platform companies. However, the application of GH strategies should align with the type of enterprise.

Digital firms, characterised by scalable digital resources and network effects, should focus on experiments aimed at exponentially increasing their user base. Conversely, traditional businesses may adopt GH strategies with different objectives, considering decreasing demand-side returns to scale.

Ultimately, GH is not a rigid process but rather a mindset and a working methodology. It involves individuals with diverse skills collaborating, supported by data, to enhance the decision-making process. This methodology establishes a continuous work loop, driven by problem-solving or specific objectives (OKR), making it a dynamic approach adaptable to the evolving business landscape. A breakdown of this is presented in Table 2.

Drawing on insights from the founder of Orangogo, we can underline the pivotal role of experimentation in optimising processes within the digital realm, particularly through the lens of GH. The constrained budget typical for many start-up initiatives makes large-scale validation efforts impractical. However, A/B testing emerges as a crucial, consistently utilised tool in this digital landscape.

Table 2. Evolution of GH.

Transformation	First Wave	Second Wave
Scope	Primarily tech start-ups	Embraced by businesses of all sizes and industries
Data Focus	Data collection for decision-making	Strong emphasis on data-driven strategies
Integration	Stand-alone GH methods	Integration with traditional marketing practices
Customer	Focus on acquisition	Expanded to include customer retention strategies
Approach	Often isolated, marketing-centric	Cross-functional approach involving multiple teams
UX	Limited emphasis on user experience	Enhanced focus on creating seamless user experience
Automation	Initial digitalisation efforts	Utilisation of automation and AI for efficiency
Experimentation	Ad hoc experimentation	Structured, continuous testing and validation

Source: Authors' elaboration.

Orangogo's strategic application of A/B testing spans across various digital marketing platforms. The practice is employed in Facebook campaigns and Google Ads, where multiple versions of the same advertisement are uploaded. Google's dynamic system then selects and displays the most effective version based on performance metrics. Similarly, Unbounce is utilised for creating several versions of a landing page, with the platform automatically showcasing the version that achieves the best results over a specified period based on pre-determined metrics.

This approach to A/B testing is not merely reactive but is also employed pre-emptively. Through the accumulated experience from past experiments, Orangogo's team can often predict the potential success of a strategy before its implementation. This predictive capacity enables a process of continuous validation, described as an 'on-the-go' validation, allowing for the constant measurement of performance. Such an approach is invaluable for swiftly determining whether a chosen direction might lead to a waste of time and resources or could potentially enhance the platform's effectiveness.

Orangogo's methodology exemplifies a dynamic and responsive approach to digital marketing and platform optimisation. By leveraging A/B testing across various digital channels and employing a strategy of continuous, experiential learning, the platform can rapidly adapt and refine its strategies. This ensures that Orangogo remains agile, minimising resource wastage while maximising potential improvements, thereby highlighting the indispensable nature of experimentation in the GH ecosystem.

3.3. DESIGN THINKING, LEAN START-UP, AGILE, AND GH

To fully grasp the nature of the growth methodology, it is necessary to explain the differences and similarities with other methodologies such as design thinking, lean start-up, and agile.

When exploring methodologies for innovation, problem-solving, and growth in today's business landscape, several approaches stand out: design thinking, lean start-up, agile, and GH. These methodologies offer distinct perspectives and processes, each with its unique strengths and areas of focus. Understanding these methodologies and their differences is crucial for organisations looking to foster innovation and adapt to evolving market trends.

3.3.1. Design Thinking

Design Thinking is fundamentally about empathy and creativity. It places a strong emphasis on understanding user problems and needs, then creatively designing solutions. Its structured process involves empathy, defining problems, ideation, prototyping, and testing. Design thinking promotes iterative prototyping and user feedback as essential elements. Design thinking is an approach that heavily utilises qualitative techniques to define customer needs, unlike agile and GH, which are more reliant on quantitative analysis.

Imagine you work for a tech company that develops smartphone applications, and you want to create a new app for task management. You've identified a problem: many existing task management apps are complex and overwhelming for users, and they often struggle to stay organised.

Step 1: Empathise

- Begin by empathising with potential users. Conduct interviews, surveys, and observations to understand their pain points, needs, and behaviours related to task management. In this phase, the buyer persona is constructed also using the empathy map, the value proposition canvas, and the customer journey.

Step 2: Define

- Define the problem based on your research. For example, you might define the problem as follows: 'Users need a task management app that is simple, intuitive, and helps them prioritize and complete tasks efficiently'.

Step 3: Ideate

- Gather a cross-functional team, including designers, developers, and product managers, for brainstorming sessions. Encourage them to generate creative ideas for the new task management app. Use techniques like brainstorming, mind mapping, or sketching.

Step 4: Prototype

- Create rough prototypes or wireframes of the app based on the most promising ideas. These can be paper sketches or digital mock-ups using design software. Keep them simple to encourage experimentation.

Step 5: Test

- Conduct usability testing with a small group of potential users. Ask them to interact with your prototypes and provide feedback. Observe how they use the app, what issues they encounter, and what features they find most valuable.

Step 6: Iterate

- Based on user feedback, refine and improve the app's design and functionality. Make necessary adjustments to address usability issues and align the app with user needs and preferences.

Step 7: Implement

- Once you have a refined prototype that meets user expectations, work with your development team to build the actual app. Ensure that the design and functionality align with the prototype.

Step 8: Launch

- Release the app to a small group of early adopters or beta testers. Monitor their feedback and make any final adjustments before the full public launch.

Step 9: Evaluate and refine

- Continuously collect user feedback and data post-launch. Use analytics tools to track user engagement and satisfaction. Make updates and improvements based on real-world usage.

This design thinking process emphasises a user-centred approach, iterative design, and continuous improvement. It allows to create of a task management app that genuinely addresses user needs and provides a user-friendly experience, increasing the chances of its success in the market.

To conclude, it is reasonable to infer that design thinking works well in a first phase of the project development, like business model validation. It can also work well for innovating specific products and services of existing companies.

3.3.2. Lean Start-up

Lean Start-up, on the other hand, prioritises the validation of business ideas and assumptions to minimise risks and resource wastage. Its core process involves building a minimum viable product (MVP), measuring its performance, and learning from user feedback. Lean start-up embraces a build–measure–learn feedback loop for continuous improvement, aiming to find product–market fit quickly. It is similar to the design thinking methodology in terms of final goal (developing a new product or service). However, it utilises different phases and approaches.

Let's get back to the previous example. You work for a tech start-up and want to create a new task management app. You're not sure if there's a market need for it, and you want to minimise the risk of building a product that users won't adopt.

Step 1: Start with a hypothesis

- Formulate a hypothesis about the problem you aim to solve and the solution you want to offer. For example, 'We believe that professionals struggle to manage their tasks efficiently using existing apps. We can solve this problem by creating a simple and intuitive task management app'.

Step 2: Build an MVP

- Develop a stripped-down version of the app with minimal features. The goal is to create something functional enough to test your hypothesis but not overly complex. This could be a basic app with task creation and completion features.

Step 3: Measure

- Launch the MVP to a small group of early adopters or a specific target audience. Use analytics tools to measure user engagement, such as the number of downloads, user interactions, and retention rates. Gather quantitative data on user behaviour.

Step 4: Learn

- Analyse the data collected from the MVP's usage. Are users adopting the app? Are they experiencing problems or challenges? Are they finding value in the features you've provided? Identify what's working and what's not.

Step 5: Pivot or persevere

- Based on what you've learned, make a decision. If the app is not gaining traction and users are not finding value, consider a pivot. This could involve changing the app's core features, target audience, or value proposition. If users are adopting it and providing positive feedback, persevere and proceed to the next steps.

Step 6: Build–measure–learn iterations

- Continue the Build–Measure–Learn cycle, making incremental improvements to the app based on user feedback and data. Gradually add new features and expand the app's functionality while closely monitoring user reactions.

The Lean Start-up methodology focusses on quickly testing the assumptions, learning from real-world feedback, and making data-driven decisions. It helps avoid extensive development efforts on a product that may not resonate with users, ultimately reducing the risk of failure.

3.3.3. Agile

Agile is an approach to project management and product development that emphasises flexibility and collaboration. Agile involves breaking work into smaller, manageable tasks and iterations, with regular review and adaptation. It encourages cross-functional teams to work closely and make decisions collectively, promoting continuous delivery and solution adaptation. In the Agile methodology, the Scrum Master plays a critical and facilitative role, acting as the bridge between the development team and the product owner, as well as ensuring that the team adheres to Agile practices. The Scrum Master is responsible for promoting and supporting Scrum by helping everyone understand Scrum theory, practices, rules, and values.

These would be the steps in the case of the task management app developed through an agile approach.

Step 1: Create a Cross-functional team

- Form a cross-functional Agile team consisting of developers, designers, testers, product managers, and other relevant stakeholders. The team should have a shared vision for the app's development.

Step 2: Create a product backlog

- Collaboratively create a prioritised product backlog, which is a list of all the features, user stories, and tasks that need to be addressed in the app. The backlog should be dynamic and adaptable.

Step 3: Sprint planning

- Plan a time-boxed development cycle called a sprint. During the sprint planning meeting, the team selects a set of items from the product backlog to work on during the upcoming sprint. These items are broken down into actionable tasks.

Step 4: Daily stand-ups

- Conduct daily stand-up meetings to keep the team informed about progress and obstacles. Each team member shares what they worked on the previous day, what they plan to work on today, and any blockers they're facing.

Step 5: Iterative development

- Begin the sprint, focussing on completing the selected backlog items. The development process is iterative, with frequent testing and feedback loops. The team aims to produce a potentially shippable product increment by the end of each sprint.

Step 6: Review and demo

- At the end of each sprint, hold a sprint review and demo. This is an opportunity for the team to showcase the work completed during the sprint to stakeholders, receive feedback, and make adjustments based on that feedback.

Step 7: Retrospective

- Conduct a sprint retrospective meeting to reflect on the sprint process. Discuss what went well, what could be improved, and what changes should be made for the next sprint. Continuous improvement is a key aspect of Agile.

Step 8: Repeat

- Repeat the sprint cycle, with each sprint building on the previous one. New backlog items are selected, developed, tested, and reviewed in subsequent sprints.

Step 9: Release

- When the product reaches a stage where it provides sufficient value to users, release it to the market. Agile allows for incremental releases, enabling you to get user feedback early in the development process.

Step 10: Feedback-driven Updates

- Even after the initial release, Agile encourages ongoing development and updates based on user feedback and changing requirements. The product evolves in response to real-world usage and user needs.

Agile methodology emphasises collaboration, adaptability, and customer feedback throughout the development process. It allows for changes and refinements to be made at any point in the project, reducing the risk of building an app that doesn't meet user expectations. Agile teams work closely together, respond to change quickly, and deliver value in short, iterative cycles.

3.3.4. Growth Hacking

GH, in contrast, focusses primarily on rapid experimentation and data-driven strategies for achieving business growth. Growth hackers employ creative and often unconventional tactics to acquire and retain users or customers. This methodology prioritises continuous testing, optimisation, and the use of key performance indicators (KPIs) to guide decision-making. Thus, we can infer that GH can be used with the other methodologies to scale the business. Hence, GH represents a valuable addition to the development and scaling of the task management app, whether it's applied during the initial development phase or after using Agile, Lean, or Design Thinking methodologies. Let's explore three hypothetical scenarios of utilising the methodology in the following exhibit.

> **Callout 7. Scenario 1: Applying GH During Initial Development (Concurrent Approach)**
>
> *Let's Say You Decide to Integrate GH from the Start of the App's Development:*
>
> 1. *Identifying the target*: use tools and framework like buyer persona, empathy map, value proposition canvas, and customer journey mapping to better develop the app and validate the product–market fit.
> 2. *Identify growth opportunities*: As you develop the app, your cross-functional team also looks for opportunities to drive user growth. For instance, you could experiment with referral mechanisms within the app to encourage users to invite their friends. This is particularly effective if the business model of the app is based on network effects.
> 3. *Implement viral features*: Integrate features that naturally encourage sharing and virality. For the task management app, this could involve allowing users to invite collaborators to tasks or projects, with incentives for referring new users.
> 4. *A/B testing*: Use A/B testing to optimise key conversion points within the app, such as the sign-up process or user onboarding. Experiment with different approaches to see which one leads to higher user acquisition and retention.
> 5. *Iterative growth*: Continuously analyse data to identify what drives growth and engagement. Adjust your GH tactics based on

real-time insights and market segmentation. For example, if you find that users who complete a certain number of tasks within the first week are more likely to become long-term users, focus on nudging users towards that milestone.

6. *Scale user base*: As you scale your user base, continue to experiment with different GH techniques and channels, such as targeted marketing campaigns or partnerships with other productivity apps.

Scenario 2: Applying GH After Agile Development (Sequential Approach)

Alternatively, you can use GH After Developing the App Using Agile:

1. *Initial agile development*: Follow the Agile methodology to develop the task management app, focussing on delivering a quality product that meets user needs. Release the initial version to a limited audience.

2. *Gather user feedback*: Collect feedback from early users to identify areas for improvement and to understand user pain points and preferences.

3. *Integration of GH*: Once you have a stable product and a user base, integrate GH techniques to accelerate user acquisition and retention. For example, you may introduce referral programmes or incentivised sharing features. The user base growth will serve to gather more data to conduct new experiments on channels and growth paths.

4. *A/B testing and optimisation*: Conduct A/B tests to optimise the app's conversion funnels, such as the upgrade to a premium subscription. Identify which strategies lead to higher CRs and revenue.

5. *Scalability*: Scale your user base by leveraging the GH strategies that have proven successful. Monitor KPIs and iterate on your approach as needed.

Scenario 3: Applying GH After Lean or Design Thinking (Sequential Approach)

Similarly, you can use GH After Applying Lean or Design Thinking Methodologies:

1. *Lean or design thinking*: Begin by using Lean or Design Thinking to create a user-centric and efficient app development process. Validate your app concept and features with real users.

2. *Initial release*: Release an MVP based on the validated concepts and features. Gather user feedback and iterate on the app's core functionality.

3. *Stable foundation*: Once you have a stable foundation, introduce GH techniques to expand your user base and improve user engagement.

4. *A/B testing and iteration*: Apply A/B testing and data-driven experimentation to fine-tune your user acquisition and retention strategies.

5. *Continuous growth*: Continue to grow your user base by scaling the tactics that yield the best results while exploring new growth opportunities.

In all scenarios, GH complements the development process by focussing on user growth, engagement, and retention. It leverages data-driven experimentation and creativity to drive the app's success in the market. Whether integrated from the start or applied sequentially, GH aims to accelerate the app's growth and adapt to changing user needs and market dynamics.

3.3.5. Integrating the Methodologies

While these methodologies have distinct focusses and processes, they share common principles that contribute to their effectiveness. All of them highlight the importance of iteration and continuous improvement based on user feedback and data analytics. They encourage cross-functional collaboration among team members, recognising that diverse perspectives enhance problem-solving. Moreover, data and metrics play pivotal roles in guiding decision-making across these methodologies.

Combining these methodologies can create a powerful approach to innovation and growth. For instance, a company can apply design thinking to deeply understand user needs and generate creative ideas. Lean start-up principles can then be employed to validate these ideas using MVPs and iterative feedback. Agile methodologies facilitate the development process, ensuring efficient and effective implementation over a series of defined stages or sprints. Finally, GH strategies can drive user acquisition and retention through creative marketing and continuous experimentation.

To sum up, while design thinking, lean start-up, agile, and GH each offer unique lenses for tackling challenges and driving growth, they are not mutually

Defining Growth Hacking

exclusive. Organisations can benefit greatly from integrating these methodologies into a holistic approach that fosters innovation, efficient development, and rapid market adoption. By doing so, they can adapt more effectively to the dynamic demands of today's business environment.

Fig. 5 represents an infographic that well explains the relationship and flow between different methodologies used in product development and business growth: Design Thinking, Lean, Agile, and GH.

The overall direction of the image shows a progression from concept to direction to problem-solving and finally to growth, illustrating how each methodology feeds into the next to move from identifying a problem to scaling a successful product in the market.

All three methodologies emphasise customer-centric approaches and rapid iteration, which are crucial for validation. Design Thinking's empathetic approach, Lean Start-up's MVP concept, and Agile's iterative development are all about understanding and meeting customer needs effectively. While not their primary strength, these methodologies can support scaling. Agile, with its focus on continuous delivery and adaptability, can help businesses scale more effectively. Lean Start-up principles, when applied correctly, can ensure that scaling efforts are always aligned with market needs. Design Thinking is inherently geared towards innovation with its creative problem-solving approach. Lean Start-up and Agile can also foster innovation by encouraging a culture of experimentation and learning from failures. Lean Start-up explicitly discusses pivoting as a response to market feedback. Agile and Design Thinking also support pivoting, as their iterative nature allows for rapid adjustments based on new insights or changing market conditions.

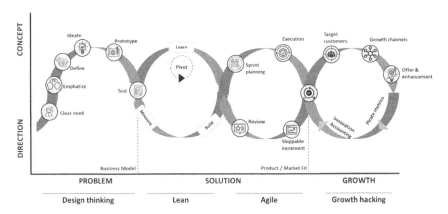

Fig. 5. Design Thinking, Lean, Agile, and Growth Hacking: Comparison of Workflows.
Source: Authors' elaboration.

Callout 8. Design Thinking, Lean, Agile, and GH: A Recap

- *Design thinking*: This methodology is shown starting with the 'Empathise' phase, where the focus is on understanding the users' needs and problems. The process continues with 'Define', where the insights from the empathise phase are used to define the clear need or problem. 'Ideate' follows, which involves brainstorming solutions to the defined problem. The next phase is 'Prototype', where ideas are turned into tangible forms. Finally, 'Test', where the prototypes are tested with users to gather feedback. This feedback could lead back to any of the previous stages for further refinement.

- *Lean*: Adjacent to Design Thinking, Lean methodology focusses on building an MVP that is then measured and learned from in iterative cycles. The 'Build' phase involves creating a simple version of the product to meet the user's basic needs. 'Measure' is where the product's success is evaluated based on user interaction. 'Learn' is the stage of gathering insights from the measurements to inform the next iteration of the product. If necessary, this may involve a 'Pivot', or a significant change in the product direction.

- *Agile*: This is depicted as a loop indicating an iterative cycle of planning, execution, and review. 'Sprint Planning' is where the team plans the work for the next short cycle, or sprint, typically lasting a few weeks. 'Execution' is the actual development work, creating a 'Shippable Increment' of the product. 'Review' involves assessing the work done during the sprint and planning for future improvements. This cycle ensures the product continues to evolve and improve rapidly, maintaining a focus on the product/market fit.

- *Growth hacking*: This phase is focussed on growth and scaling the product after achieving product/market fit. It begins with targeting customers and identifying growth channels to reach them. 'Offer & Enhancement' involves refining the product offer and making enhancements based on user feedback and market demand. 'Innovation Accounting' and 'Pirate Metrics' (also known as AARRR: Acquisition, Activation, Retention, Revenue, and Referral) are used to measure the effectiveness of growth strategies and tactics.

GH is particularly effective in scaling because it combines aspects of marketing, analytics, and technology to achieve rapid growth. Its focus on measurable and scalable tactics makes it ideal for expanding a business's reach quickly. Though primarily associated with scaling, GH can also be applied to other aspects. For instance, its data-driven approach can assist in validating market assumptions. In terms of innovation, the creative and unconventional strategies typical of GH can lead to innovative solutions. Similarly, its flexibility and focus on measurable results can be valuable when a business needs to pivot.

The real power lies in the integration of these methodologies. For instance, combining the customer-centric approach of Design Thinking with the data-driven tactics of GH can lead to both innovative and scalable business models. Similarly, the principles of Lean Start-up can be interwoven with Agile methodologies to create a robust framework for both validating and rapidly iterating on a business model (Silva et al., 2020).

In summary, while each methodology has areas where it excels, their principles can be applied across all stages of a business model's lifecycle. GH stands out in scaling but can also contribute significantly to innovation and pivoting (Bargoni, Santoro, et al., 2024; Bargoni, Smrčka, et al., 2024; Troisi et al., 2020). The key is to understand the core principles of each methodology and adapt them to the specific challenges and opportunities of each stage in the business model's evolution.

NOTES

1. In the context of platforms and technology, a network effect, also known as a network externality or Metcalfe's law, refers to the phenomenon where the value of a product, service, or platform increases exponentially as the number of users or participants grows. In essence, the more people who use the platform, the more valuable it becomes to each user. A network effect occurs when each new user of the platform adds value to the existing users and, in turn, benefits from the value created by those users. This positive feedback loop can lead to exponential growth and a self-reinforcing cycle of increasing adoption.

4

PRACTISING GROWTH

ABSTRACT

This chapter discusses strategic management and growth hacking as complementary approaches to achieving organisational goals and driving growth. It emphasises the importance of aligning growth hacking efforts with overall corporate strategy to ensure synergy and effectiveness. Exploring various aspects of strategic management, including vision, goals, environmental analysis, strategy formulation, implementation, and performance monitoring, the authors delve into the integration of growth hacking with strategic management, highlighting key points of alignment such as resource allocation, target market segmentation, brand consistency, data alignment, risk management, and integration with other functions.

Keywords: Strategic management; growth hacking; business model innovation; growth steps; experimentation; growth team

4.1. STRATEGIC MANAGEMENT. DEFINING THE PATH FORWARD

Strategy, within the context of organisational management, is the deliberate and systematic plan of action designed to achieve specific long-term goals and objectives. It encompasses the identification of critical factors, allocation of resources, and coordination of efforts to align with an organisation's mission, vision, and values (Ansoff, 2007; Santoro, 2019).

Strategic management, on the other hand, is the comprehensive process of formulating, implementing, and evaluating these strategies to steer an organisation towards its desired future state. It serves as a guiding framework that ensures the organisation operates cohesively towards its overarching goals and objectives.

Key elements of strategic management include:

- *Vision and mission*: An organisation's vision paints a compelling picture of its long-term aspirations, while the mission statement defines its purpose and the value it aims to deliver to stakeholders.
- *Goals and objectives*: Goals represent high-level, qualitative statements outlining what the organisation seeks to achieve. Objectives, on the other hand, are specific, measurable, and time-bound targets that serve as the foundation for achieving these goals.
- *Environmental analysis*: The strategic management process begins with an in-depth examination of both the internal strengths and weaknesses of the organisation, as well as the external opportunities and threats it faces. Tools such as SWOT analysis help in this assessment.
- *Strategy formulation*: This phase involves the careful development of strategies and action plans that align with the organisation's vision, mission, and goals. Various strategic approaches, such as cost leadership, differentiation, and focus, are considered.
- *Strategy implementation*: The execution of chosen strategies involves the allocation of resources, the establishment of organisational structures, and the effective implementation of plans.
- *Performance monitoring*: A critical aspect of strategic management is the continuous evaluation of progress against objectives. Key performance indicators (KPIs) are used to track performance and adjust as necessary.

The link between strategic management and growth hacking is vital and highly synergistic. As anticipated, strategic management provides the overall vision, goals, and direction of a company, while growth hacking offers agile and innovative methods to achieve these goals, especially in terms of customer acquisition and market growth. As a consequence, it is necessary to align the growth efforts with overall business goals. In this sense, growth hacking efforts must align with the company's broader goals. This alignment ensures that the tactics employed by growth hacking teams contribute significantly to the company's long-term vision and goals, such as market expansion, revenue growth, or brand positioning. The growth hacking team, therefore, will need to follow the overall corporate strategy to define tactics and experiments. However, as already pointed out, growth hacking is an agile and lean methodology that often leads to changing strategic philosophy and innovating the business model.

Hence, in an increasingly dynamic competitive environment, the corporate management team will need to interface with the growth team to possibly change the strategic philosophy in an agile way. In other words, the company's strategy may change based on the work of the growth team around six pivotal points:

(1) *Resource allocation*: Strategic management determines the allocation of resources among different departments and initiatives. Growth hacking teams must work within these parameters, making efficient use of allocated resources (budget, personnel, technology) to experiment and implement growth tactics. In other words, corporate finance sets the budget for the growth team, which then must operate through experiments and projects while adhering to the budget.

(2) *Target market and customer segmentation*: The company's strategic plan often outlines the target market and key customer segments. Growth hackers must tailor their strategies to these segments, ensuring that growth hacking initiatives resonate with the intended audience and effectively attract and retain customers. However, as discussed previously, experiments may highlight the need to focus on a new target market or develop a new product. Again, from a strategic perspective, corporate management will need to follow the insights of the growth team to change strategy accordingly.

(3) *Brand consistency*: Although growth hacking often involves creative and unconventional tactics, it is essential that these efforts be consistent with the company's brand identity and values. Strategic management sets the tone in which the brand is presented and perceived, and growth hacking activities must reinforce, not contradict, the brand image. This is especially true for changing viral and guerrilla marketing.

(4) *Data and metrics alignment*: KPIs and metrics used to evaluate the success of growth hacking should be chosen based on their relevance to the company's strategic goals. This alignment ensures that the growth hacking team focusses on the metrics that are truly important to the overall success of the company. In short, corporate objectives and key results (OKRs) must be consistent with the growth team's OKRs.

(5) *Risk management*: Strategic management involves assessing and managing risk. Growth hacking strategies, known for rapid experimentation, must be developed by understanding the level of risk acceptable to the company. This approach ensures that the tactics chosen do not expose the company to excessive risk or potential reputational damage.

(6) *Integration with other functions*: Growth hacking should not operate in isolation but rather in concert with other business functions such as product development, marketing, sales, and customer service. The company's strategic plan often outlines the interrelationship between these different functions, and growth hacking initiatives must integrate and support these interdependencies. Often, large organisations create growth teams made up precisely of employees from existing functions. This allows for varied expertise and breaks down silos.

Callout 9. Strategic Management and Growth Hacking: Integrating a Bottom Up Approach with Corporate Strategy

In this interview, Alessia Camera, a growth hacker with 15 years of experience in digital marketing primarily developed in early-stage start-ups in London explains how the managing of a growth hacking team must align with the corporate strategy of the firm.

What Is Growth Hacking to You, and How Would You Define It?

For me, growth hacking emerged from my experiences in 2012/2013 with start-ups; I began with the 100 people working in the start-up ecosystem in London to understand that traditional digital marketing principles didn't make much sense in that environment. For a start-up, it makes sense to launch an app without having large budgets available; it makes sense to be focussed on the users, trying to understand their needs and the value they can get from the app and, on the other hand, it also makes sense to be focussed on budgets in terms of performance, since the goal of any start-up is to gain traction.

Could You Share Recent Growth Hacking Practices at Taxfix?

I joined Taxfix in February 2021 and not much experimentation work had been done; we must keep in mind that Taxfix faces complications mainly because, in Italy, digitalisation among people is still low, moreover talking about taxes is a taboo subject, and third, it deals with a latent need, doing tax returns is not a priority for people.

When I joined the team I did two things: the first was to create an experimentation framework, to create experimentation processes that created routines for the team; for example, working on creatives on Facebook, testing them for two weeks, creating ways to identify a definition of assets.

On one hand, we had this framework then we started working on the product, because in 2021 Taxfix was launching a mobile version and the web version, only that when the app was downloaded the only thing the user could do was the tax return; there was a lack of activation moment, a moment when people after downloading the app, therefore after the acquisition moment, understand that they can actually relate to the product before reaching the payment moment.

From my point of view, this moment was missing, which usually corresponds to the 'wow' moment when people understand that the service meets their needs; I therefore liaised with the product team to try to create it and we decided to test what among the hypotheses was the simplest and most immediate way, because then we only had 7 months since taxes can only be done from February to September.

In What Time Horizon Do You Use These Initiatives?

Having a six-month season, we always strive to deliver results that are specific to that season; these tests were conducted to gather learnings for 2022. Then, of course, once you launch experiments, you can understand if there's a possibility they can be optimised. For instance, it's true that to see the results you need to wait at least six months, but by feeding Google's algorithm the link directly, it's still possible to gain insights.

For instance, it's true that before having some results you need to wait at least six months (until the end of the season), but by directly feeding Google's algorithm it's still possible to gain some insights.

Do the Objectives of Growth Hacking Align with Those of the Company, or Are Specific Objectives Set?

In my opinion, they must be aligned with those of the company, in the sense that doing growth hacking means growing the company, and growing the company means helping it improve revenue, user numbers, or average revenue per user (ARPU); there must be metrics that define the business value.

It's true that there are growth hacking initiatives more related to learning, helping the team understand what to do, but this phase then needs to eventually connect to the revenue objectives of the companies.

Can You Think of Other Benefits, in Terms of Secondary Objectives and the Necessary Resources to Achieve Them, Encountered After the Application of Growth Hacking?

Fundamentally, it's the people; there's a need to create a cross-functional team; within the team, there's a need for those who do marketing, performance marketing, product design, or web design. An example is engineers who work in the app so that there can be fixes that are done in-app, to better connect product and marketing. There's a need for copywriting, and so on. So, in my opinion, these are the compositions of people that must be there within the team.

On the investment side, it depends. There can be tests that are done on a zero budget and tests where a budget is necessary. What makes sense to consider is speed because when there are budgets what impacts is being faster to bring home results, compared to going organic.

As for other benefits, for example, in Taxfix, I've seen a strong change in speed; putting together a cross-functional team that works on experiments brings home learnings in a few weeks, allows you to go much faster because you work on a series of hypotheses, you understand which experiment you want to launch and through the data then the direction to take; it allows to go fast and not get stuck in decision-making loops.

This approach is very data-driven and allows on one hand to optimise results, on the other, obviously doesn't give sensational answers, it might also give a very small insight on what to continue experimentation on, but in general, it allows you to go fast and understand what the objective is.

Earlier You Mentioned That There Are Difficulties in Your Sector, Maybe Both in a Growth Hacking Environment and at a Corporate Level?

Yes, the difficulties we have are related to the fact that we work in a very particular sector, where people either don't know things or don't want to know them, but this is a problem for all companies operating in a sector where there isn't a real problem felt among people; this could be complicated because you have to start thinking a bit differently since selling an app that does tax returns is different from selling a dish for the home with an e-commerce made by Italian designers, this obviously makes certain businesses more complex and the application of growth hacking on some of them challenging.

The other complication is related to the mindset of people, including both executives and teams; unfortunately, there's still too much of an idea that marketing does marketing and product does product. This approach nowadays makes no sense, especially when we talk about innovative products; what marketing needs to do is certainly distribute them, but I wouldn't say that's the only goal of marketing.

The problem is that when this discussion stays within the team, it leads to getting lost in philosophies and principles that don't lead anywhere, worse if these conversations also reach the upper levels, because they obviously bring friction and lead to top-down approaches that do not help.

Growth hacking is a bottom-up approach; the team does things and then brings insights to the executives for decision-making. If the executives make decisions, without being in line with the data-driven results of the experiments, this leads to endless inefficiencies.

4.2. RYAN HOLIDAY'S FOUR GROWTH STEPS

This chapter aims to shed light on how firms can put in practice the growth process. One of the most common methods is the four-stage approach. In this sense, Ryan Holiday, a well-known marketing strategist and author, outlines a four-step process for growth, particularly focussing on how businesses can effectively market and grow their brand (Holiday, 2014). These steps are based on his extensive experience in marketing and are designed to be both practical and impactful. Here's a brief overview of Ryan Holiday's four growth steps:

4.2.1. Product–Market Fit

The first stage in the growth hacking journey is to ensure that there is an appropriate alignment between the product and the target market, which is known as product–market fit. This is not just about internal innovation but about responding to a compelling market demand. For example, Slack, initially a tool developed for internal team communication, found a universal demand for streamlined communication in teams and businesses, leading to widespread adoption. The purpose of this phase is to ensure that the product aligns as closely as possible with market demands, addressing the perceived pain points of the customer and meeting their sought-after benefits. Therefore, a comprehensive analysis of consumer behaviour and needs is essential. In this regard, the value proposition canvas illustrated and explained in Chapter 1 can be very useful.

4.2.2. Finding the 'Hack'

The second phase is about identifying the right 'hack' that enables efficient targeting of the right customers in a cost-effective manner. Uber excelled in this phase by handing out free ride coupons at tech conferences, tapping directly into a tech-savvy audience that would appreciate and adopt a mobile-based ride-sharing service. Similarly, LinkedIn offered users the ability to upload their entire email contact list to connect with associates, exponentially increasing their user base with minimal effort. SEM strategies also fall under this category. In other words, this phase aims to sell the right product to the right target audience (product–market fit), in the right place (physical or virtual), through the right channel, at the right time (such as a particular time of day or specific day of the week). To adhere to this principle, one must address the question: which strategy allows to maximise the conversion rate as much as possible?

Callout 10. The Noble Art of Hacking

The 'hack' phase is a critical component of growth hacking strategies, focussing on optimising and fine-tuning the approach to selling a product or service. This phase is all about precision and effectiveness, ensuring that the value proposition reaches the right audience, at the right time, and through the most suitable channels. Here's a brief overview of what this entails:

- *Selling the right product*: This involves ensuring that the product or service perfectly aligns with the needs, desires, and pain points of the target market. It's about offering a solution that genuinely addresses a significant problem or fulfils a need for the customer. It is extremely related to the concept of product-market fit (PFM) as explained above.

- *To the right target*: Identifying and understanding the target audience is crucial. This means having a deep knowledge of who the potential customers are, including their demographics, behaviours, preferences, and the channels they frequent.

- *At the right moment*: Timing can significantly impact the success of a product launch or marketing campaign. This involves understanding the customer's journey and recognising the most opportune moments to introduce the product or make an offer.

- *In the right place*: Placement is about choosing the most effective channels to reach the target audience, whether it's through physical places, social media, email marketing, search engine optimisation (SEO), or other digital platforms. The goal is to be where the customers are and where they are most likely to engage with the product.

The hack phase is thus a strategic exercise in targeting and optimisation, leveraging data and insights to make informed decisions that enhance the product's market fit and adoption rate. It requires a blend of creativity, analytics, and experimentation to find the most efficient paths to growth.

There are numerous tools available to support the hack phase, each designed to optimise different facets of your strategy, from understanding your audience to executing targeted campaigns. Tools such as Google Analytics enable tracking of user behaviour to gain a deeper understanding of both current and potential consumers, thereby refining your target demographic. Mixpanel extends these capabilities by providing advanced analytics for mobile and web, with a particular focus on user interaction, while Heap offers the advantage of capturing every user action on your website or app automatically, enabling a detailed analysis without the need to predefine tracking parameters.

For collecting customer feedback and insights, SurveyMonkey is an invaluable tool that allows the creation and distribution of surveys. Hotjar goes a step further by integrating analytics and feedback tools, offering a comprehensive understanding of how users interact with your website. Similarly, Typeform enhances user engagement through its interactive surveys and forms.

Email marketing and automation campaigns can be significantly optimised using tools like Mailchimp, an all-in-one marketing platform that facilitates communication with clients and customers. HubSpot offers a complete suite of software for marketing, sales, and customer service, including a fully free Customer Relationship Management (CRM). Autopilot caters to marketing automation across email, SMS, and direct mail, streamlining communication strategies.

SEO and content marketing efforts are bolstered by tools such as Ahrefs, which aids in keyword research, competitor analysis, and site audits. SEMRush enhances online visibility and provides marketing insights, while Moz helps increase traffic, rankings, and visibility in search results with its comprehensive SEO software and data.

Customer data platforms are effective tools that help businesses collect, clean, and control their customer data. For example, Twilio Segment allows companies to gather data from various sources (like websites, mobile apps, CRMs, and other online platforms) into a single repository. With the data collected, Segment allows businesses to create detailed segments based on user behaviour, demographics, and custom events. Segment processes data in real time, enabling businesses to react quickly to customer actions. This capability allows for dynamic targeting and personalisation, adjusting marketing strategies as customer behaviours change. With the ability to segment audiences and track their behaviour, Segment enables businesses to run A/B tests and experiments to determine the most effective strategies for engaging their target audience. This data-driven approach ensures that marketing efforts are optimised based on actual user response.

Integrating these tools into growth hacking strategies can significantly improve the ability to hack the growth process, allowing to sell the right product to the right target, at the right moment, and in the right place. By leveraging the specific strengths of each tool, companies can craft a finely tuned approach to growth that is both data-driven and customer-focussed, ensuring that the product not only meets but exceeds market expectations.

4.2.3. Harnessing Virality

The third phase focusses on creating a viral loop through digital channels, particularly social media. A notable example is Twitter, which gained traction at the South by Southwest (SXSW) conference when they displayed live tweets on screens around the venue, showcasing the platform's real-time communication capabilities and encouraging attendees to join in the conversation. Many platforms subject to network effects often rely on referral programmes, where active users are incentivised to bring in other users to receive cash and non-cash rewards. For example, Dropbox implemented a referral programme that rewarded both the referrer and the new user. When a user referred someone to Dropbox, and that person signed up through the referral link, both the referrer and the new user received additional storage space for free. This 'give one, get one' approach incentivised users to refer others and contributed to Dropbox's rapid growth. Uber's referral programme offered existing users a referral code to share with friends and family. When a new user signed up using the referral code and completed their first ride, both the existing user and the new user received a credit or discount on future rides. This encouraged existing users to invite new riders to the platform, expanding Uber's customer base. Airbnb's referral programme encouraged hosts and guests to refer friends to the platform. When a referred friend completed their first stay or hosted their first guest, both the referrer and the new user received travel credits. This incentivised Airbnb's community members to bring new hosts and guests into the platform, fuelling its growth.

> **Callout 11. Different Types of Virality**
>
> Each type of virality leverages different aspects of user behaviour and technology platforms to spread a product or service. The effectiveness of these viral strategies can depend on various factors, including the product's market fit, the user base's engagement level, and the overall execution of the viral mechanisms.
>
> **Inherent Virality**
>
> Inherent virality occurs when the use of a product or service naturally encourages spreading to others. This type of virality is built into the product's core functionality. For example, a messaging app becomes more valuable as more friends and family join, encouraging users to invite others.
>
> **Social Virality**
>
> Social virality involves content or products becoming viral through social networks and platforms. This can happen organically, where users share content because it resonates with them or fits within current trends, amplifying the product's visibility through likes, shares, and comments.

> **Incentivised Virality**
>
> Incentivised virality happens when users are offered rewards for sharing the product or service with others. For instance, a cloud storage service might offer extra storage space for each new user an existing customer refers. This type of virality motivates users to spread the word in exchange for tangible benefits.
>
> **Engineered Virality**
>
> Engineered virality refers to deliberate strategies designed to encourage users to share a product or a service. This can include the integration of share buttons within a product, making it easy for users to share content or invite others to the platform. It often involves analysing user behaviour to create features that facilitate and encourage sharing at optimal points in the user experience.

4.2.4. Data-driven Customer Retention

In the fourth phase, growth hacking emphasises enhancing customer retention through data-driven CRM and optimising marketing activities. For instance, Amazon uses sophisticated algorithms to show personalised recommendations, thereby increasing repeat purchases. Netflix takes it a step further by not only recommending content based on viewing habits but also by using data to drive the creation of new content, ensuring that their offerings have a higher chance of retaining viewers. As previously mentioned, Duolingo, with the goal of language learning, aims to increase the daily active user rate and consequently optimise retention.

By leveraging these strategies, growth hackers guide products through the lifecycle from concept to loyal customer base, employing inventive tactics at each stage to fuel rapid growth.

> **Callout 12. Product–Market Fit: The Imaginary Case of TaskFlow**
>
> In the bustling landscape of small- to medium-sized businesses, TaskFlow emerged as an innovative productivity app that seamlessly integrates task management, communication, and project tracking into a single platform. The genesis of TaskFlow was marked by a keen observation: businesses

were cobbling together disparate tools to manage their daily operations. Through meticulous market research and iterative beta testing with actual businesses, TaskFlow was meticulously crafted to alleviate common operational inefficiencies, ensuring a genuine product–market fit.

The Strategic 'Hack': Penetrating the Market

Recognising the need for an unconventional market entry, TaskFlow pinpointed networking events and co-working spaces as fertile grounds for its introduction. An offer was extended: a complimentary premium subscription for three months to businesses registering on the spot. TaskFlow also courted social media influencers in the productivity domain, leveraging their platforms for live app demonstrations, thus amplifying reach and credibility among potential users. SEM tactics were also implemented to exploit the potential of google search engine system.

Harnessing Virality: A Competitive Edge

TaskFlow ingeniously baked virality into its user experience. The app's standout feature, a public leader board, showcased the most productive teams and individuals each month. This gamification encouraged users to share their achievements on social media, transforming each user's success into a testament to the app's efficacy. A clever referral programme further galvanised user engagement, offering enhanced features as rewards for user-driven growth.

Data-driven Retention: Cultivating Loyalty

To convert initial user engagement into enduring loyalty, TaskFlow harnessed the power of data analytics. The app delivered customised productivity insights and engaged users with unexplored features. A loyalty programme further anchored users to TaskFlow, offering subscription incentives to those with long-term commitments. By prioritising user-suggested features in its development roadmap, TaskFlow fostered a community-centric ethos, ensuring that the voices of its users were not just heard but acted upon.

TaskFlow's strategic navigation through the growth hacking phases cultivated a robust user base, setting the stage for a compelling narrative of innovation, market acuity, and enduring user engagement.

4.3. PIRATE FUNNEL

The Pirate Funnel (see Fig. 6), a cornerstone concept in growth hacking, was introduced by Dave McClure, a prominent American entrepreneur and angel investor, in 2007 (McClure, 2007). This strategic framework is termed the 'Pirate Funnel' due to its AAARRR acronym, which stands for Awareness, Acquisition, Activation, Retention, Revenue, and Referral. Designed as a navigational tool, the Pirate Funnel provides a structured approach to understanding and optimising the relationship between a product or service and its customers, along a precise funnel representing the customer journey.

Typically, the Pirate Funnel comprises six stages, though they are adaptable to the unique dynamics of each business. The Pirate Funnel is not just about outlining the customer journey; it's about optimising it and developing specific strategies. In other terms, the funnel's structure is a blueprint for action (see Table 3). At each stage, businesses must ask critical questions and develop corresponding tactics. Then, for each stage, businesses should define specific KPIs to measure the effectiveness of their strategies. These KPIs provide actionable insights and allow companies to make data-driven decisions.

- *Awareness KPIs* might include SEO reach and/or impression, keywords visibility, cost per 1,000 impressions, cost per click.
- *Acquisition KPIs* might include cost per acquisition (CPA), customer acquisition cost (CAC), website traffic sources, and conversion rates.
- *Activation KPIs* could be the percentage of users taking a desired action upon their first visit.
- *Retention KPIs* may involve tracking daily or monthly active users and churn rates.

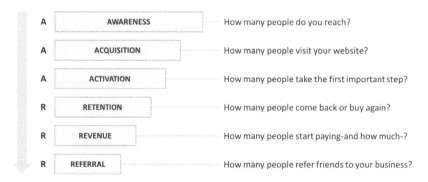

Fig. 6. Pirate Funnel.
Source: Authors' elaboration based on McClure (2007). Start-up metrics for pirates.

Practising Growth 77

Table 3. Operationalising the Stages of the Pirate Funnel.

Stages of the Pirate Funnel	Dynamics of the Business	Critical Questions to Develop the Tactics	KPIs	Operationalising KPIs
Awareness	This stage involves creating brand or product visibility within the target market	How do we create visibility for our product? Strategies might include content marketing, SEO, or partnerships	Impression and reach analysis	Impressions = the number of times the insertion has been displayed on social media platforms. Reach = number of users exposed to the adv. A low number might indicate a visibility issue
			Click Through Rate (CTR)	Represents the ratio of clicks to the number of impressions. A high CTR indicates that the content is engaging and prompts action. For example, if a banner receives a thousand impressions and ten clicks, the CTR would be 1%. If another banner receives a hundred impressions and ten clicks, the CTR would be 10%, indicating a higher performance and a greater propensity to drive action
Acquisition	This is the process by which potential customers are first brought to the product. It's where awareness turns into interest	What channels bring in the most users? Tactic development can range from PPC campaigns to influencer collaborations	Website or Web App Bounce Rate	This metric indicates the 'age of visitors who leave a website or web application after viewing only one page, which can signal the level of interest generated by the site or app. A high bounce rate might suggest the need for better engagement strategies or improvements in targeting
			Cost per acquisition (CPA)	CPA is a key performance metric that measures the total cost of acquiring a new customer through a specific channel or campaign. It encompasses all marketing and advertising expenses involved in convincing a potential customer to complete a purchase or a desired action, divided by the number of new customers acquired as a result of those efforts

(Continued)

Table 3. Operationalising the Stages of the Pirate Funnel. *(Continued)*

Stages of the Pirate Funnel	Dynamics of the Business	Critical Questions to Develop the Tactics	KPIs	Operationalising KPIs
			Number of Downloads	In the context of apps, the number of downloads represents a direct metric of customer acquisition, especially if the app is linked to a service or store like the App Store or Google Play Store
Activation	In this stage, customers have their first meaningful interaction with the product, experiencing its core value proposition	How do we ensure the first user experience highlights the product's value? Tactics may involve onboarding improvements or trial offers	Sign-up Rate to Download Ratio	This KPI measures the conversion rate from app downloads to actual sign-ups or subscriptions, an essential metric for understanding how well the app retains users post-download
			Email List Growth	The increase in the number of email subscribers indicates interest and potential for further engagement. A slow growth rate might point to the need for better promotional strategies or more compelling lead magnets
Retention	This phase focusses on keeping customers engaged and using the product over time	What keeps customers coming back? Strategies could be product updates, community building, or responsive customer support	Churn rate	A critical KPI in subscription-based services, churn rate measures the percentage of customers who stop using the service over a certain period. A high churn rate can be a significant concern, indicating issues with long-term value or customer satisfaction
			Repeat Purchase Rate	This KPI is particularly important for e-commerce and retail, measuring the percentage of customers who make more than one purchase. It's a direct indicator of customer loyalty and the effectiveness of retention strategies

Revenue	The funnel turns usage into monetary value, signifying when customers start paying for the product or the service	How do we optimise the conversion of users into paying customers? Tactics might include pricing strategies, upselling, or bundling offers	Lifetime Value (LTV)	This KPI indicates the total revenue generated by a single customer over the course of their relationship with a company. For example, if a customer makes a yearly purchase of 500€ for 10 years on an e-commerce platform, their LTV would be 5,000€. Understanding LTV is critical for determining how much a company can afford to spend on acquiring each new customer, considering the acquisition and switching costs involved
			Average Revenue Per User (ARPU)	This refers to the average revenue generated per user. It's a more precise metric than LTV because it can indicate the performance of different customer segments. For instance, if there were 1,000 customers who generated a total end-year revenue of 10,000€, the ARPU would be 10€ per customer. However, this doesn't provide insights into which customers are the top performers
			Monthly Recurring Revenue (MRR)	MRR measures the predictable monthly income that a company expects to receive. It is a crucial metric for businesses with subscription models as it provides a clear view of steady cash flow
Referral	In this phase, satisfied customers become advocates, referring new users and thus continuing the growth cycle	How do we encourage users to refer others? Referral programmes or social sharing incentives can be effective tactics here	Net Promoter Score (NPS)	NPS is the leading metric for measuring customer satisfaction and loyalty. It gauges the likelihood of customers recommending a product or service to others. Customers are asked how likely they are to recommend a product, service, or company on a scale of 0–10. Respondents are categorised as promoters (9–10 rating), passives (7–8 rating), or detractors (0–6 rating). The NPS is calculated as the percentage of promoters minus the percentage of detractors, multiplied by 100

(Continued)

Table 3. Operationalising the Stages of the Pirate Funnel. *(Continued)*

Stages of the Pirate Funnel	Dynamics of the Business	Critical Questions to Develop the Tactics	KPIs	Operationalising KPIs
			Viral Coefficient (*K*-factor)	This indicates the potential for virality of a product or service and is primarily calculated in referral systems where one user can invite others through invitation links. The viral coefficient is calculated as the number of invites sent by each user multiplied by the conversion rate of each invite. If, for example, 500 users send out 10 invites each, and 20% of these invites result in new sign-ups, the viral coefficient would be 1.0, indicating that each user brings in one additional user on average, a sign of a potentially viral product
			Number of Conversions via Referral	Although not mentioned as critical as other metrics, this KPI can help analyse the referral rate. It measures the number of new users or customers acquired through each referral, contributing to an understanding of the engagement on social media

Source: Authors' elaboration.

- *Revenue KPIs* could look at the ARPU and lifetime value (LTV).
- *Referral KPIs* might assess the viral coefficient or the number of new users brought in by referrals. Also, net-promoter score (NPS) is widely used.

4.4. OKRS-DRIVEN GROWTH

OKRs is a goal-setting framework that help organisations define goals (objectives) and track the outcomes (key results). The method was originally developed by Intel and has been widely popularised by companies like Google for its effectiveness in setting and communicating clear goals and results throughout an organisation.

In today's setting, where numerous companies permit their employees to work from any location, leading to a transformation in how employees coordinate their tasks and unite around shared objectives, OKRs serve as a goal-setting framework. OKR was formulated to enhance organisational efficiency and effectiveness in achieving business goals by fostering employee engagement and facilitating decision-making (Niven & Lamorte, 2016). The framework offers advantages such as focus and regular priority establishment. Implementing OKR fosters inter-team transparency, allowing teams to align cross-functionally and enhance product development (Berntzen et al., 2022; Doerr, 2018; Wodtke, 2016). Objectives are set for a specific duration, and key results are defined to ensure consistent progress towards these objectives through specific tasks. An objective concisely articulates what the team aims to achieve, with a well-defined target achievable within three months and reflecting the team's collective vision. Key results are quantifiable metrics enabling the team to track progress and ascertain whether a specific objective has been achieved.

What do OKRs stand for?

- *Objectives*: These are significant, concrete, action-oriented, and (ideally) inspirational goals. They are designed to propel the organisation in a desired direction. Objectives should be short, memorable, and engaging. They are qualitative and indicate what one wants to achieve.
- *Key results*: These are measures that monitor how and whether we meet the objectives. They are quantifiable, making it clear whether the objective has been achieved with a simple success or fail. They should be aggressive yet realistic, with evidence-based benchmarks and milestones that can track progress towards the objective.

The process of OKR typically follows a cadence (quarterly, annually, etc.) and encourages regular check-ins to track progress, create alignment, and encourage engagement across teams. OKRs are often public within the organisation to ensure transparency and alignment.

The key benefits of OKRs include:

- Focussing efforts on what truly matters.
- Aligning and connecting team and individual work to company-wide goals.
- Driving engagement through participation in goal setting.
- Encouraging risk-taking and innovation by setting challenging targets.

The OKR framework is flexible and can be adapted for organisations of different sizes and industries to help them set, communicate, and monitor their progress towards their strategic goals.

The OKR methodology can be particularly powerful when applied to growth hacking and similar methodologies focussed on rapid growth and scalability (Bargoni, Smrčka, et al., 2024). Here's how OKRs can be integrated:

(1) *Defining clear growth objectives:*

- OKRs enable growth hackers to define clear and ambitious goals that are aligned with the company's vision for growth. For instance, an objective might be 'Expand into two new international markets' or 'Grow the user base by 50%'.

(2) *Setting measurable key results*:

- For each growth objective, specific, measurable key results are set to track progress. In growth hacking, these could include metrics such as 'Increase the number of active users from X to Y' or 'Achieve a Z% conversion rate on new sign-ups'.

(3) *Aligning team efforts*:

- Growth hacking often involves cross-functional teams. OKRs help to align these diverse teams towards common growth targets, ensuring that marketing, product development, sales, and other departments work synergistically.

(4) *Encouraging experimentation*:

- The OKR framework supports a culture of experimentation intrinsic to growth hacking. Teams can set objectives related to testing new growth tactics and then define key results that measure the success of these experiments.

(5) *Iterating quickly*:

- OKRs are reviewed regularly (often quarterly), which dovetails with the rapid iteration cycles of growth hacking. This allows teams to pivot quickly if certain strategies aren't working, or to double down on successful tactics.

(6) *Fostering transparency and accountability*:

- By making OKRs visible to all team members, everyone becomes aware of the growth goals and their role in achieving them. This transparency fosters a sense of ownership and accountability, which is crucial in a fast-paced growth environment.

(7) *Data-driven decision-making*:

- Key results in OKRs are based on data. This emphasis on metrics and analytics meshes well with the data-driven approach of growth hacking, where decisions are made based on what the data indicate about user behaviour and market trends.

For example, a growth hacking team might set an OKR around improving the user onboarding process to increase engagement. The objective could be 'Revamp the onboarding experience to improve user engagement'. Key results to measure this might include 'Increase the percentage of users who complete the onboarding process by X%', 'Achieve a Y% reduction in new user drop-off within the first week', and 'Increase average session duration by Z%'.

In this way, OKRs can provide a structured framework to set goals, measure progress, and drive the iterative, innovative efforts that are at the heart of growth hacking.

4.5. THE EXPERIMENTATION PROCESS

As highlighted by recent literature, growth is an approach that can be utilised by all types of companies, across all sectors and contexts (Bargoni, Santoro, et al., 2024). Although it has been associated with the world of platforms and start-ups, its effectiveness has recently been tested in other contexts as well. In this scenario, there is an experimentation process that all businesses and organisations can utilise. This process is based on four specific phases: goal or problem definition; idea generation; prioritisation; and execution.

(1) *Goal or problem definition*: This initial phase involves clearly identifying the specific goal to be achieved or the problem that needs to be solved. It sets the direction for the experimentation process, ensuring that all efforts are aligned with addressing a concrete challenge or objective. In this phase, it is essential to carry out an analysis process to define macro-objectives (e.g. improving performance) or micro-objectives (e.g. resolving specific customer issues). This analysis could involve consumer behaviour, comparison with customer care, analysis of metrics or KPIs, re-evaluation of the buyer persona, analysis of the business model, analysis of the value proposition in relation to the target market, analysis of the user experience, mapping, and analysis of the AAARRR funnels, competitor analysis, and so on (Gaito, 2017).

(2) *Idea generation*: Once the goal or problem is defined, the next step is to brainstorm potential solutions or strategies. This phase encourages creativity and open thinking, allowing the team to come up with a diverse set of ideas that could potentially address the identified goal or problem. In this phase, it is vital to involve as many stakeholders as possible, both internal and external.

(3) *Prioritisation*: After generating a list of ideas, the team must then prioritise which ideas to test based on factors such as potential impact, feasibility, and resources required. This step is crucial for focussing efforts on the most promising experiments, ensuring efficient use of time and resources. The ICE method is a prioritisation technique used to evaluate and select ideas based on three criteria: Impact, Confidence, and Ease. Here's a description of each component:

- *Impact*: This criterion assesses the potential effect or benefit an idea or initiative could have if successfully implemented. The impact is measured in terms of the positive change or value it would bring to the company, such as increased revenue, improved customer satisfaction, or enhanced product functionality. Ideas with a higher potential impact are generally prioritised over those with lesser impact.

- *Confidence*: Confidence evaluates how certain you are about your assessments of both the impact and the ease of implementation. It reflects the level of evidence or data supporting the predicted effects of an idea. Higher confidence levels indicate a stronger belief in the idea's success based on available data, research, or previous experiences. Confidence helps to mitigate the risk of investing in unproven or speculative initiatives.

- *Ease (or Effort)*: This criterion examines how easy or difficult it would be to implement the idea. It considers the required resources, time, and effort needed to execute the initiative. Ideas that are easier to implement, requiring fewer resources or less time, often receive higher priority, especially when resources are limited.

Each idea is scored against these three criteria on a scale (often from 1 to 10), and then an overall ICE score is calculated, typically by taking the average of the three scores. The ideas with the highest ICE scores are considered top priorities for implementation, as they are expected to deliver the most significant impact, have a high level of confidence, and are relatively easier to execute compared to other options. The ICE method provides a structured and quantitative approach to idea selection, helping teams to make informed decisions by balancing the potential benefits against the likelihood of success and the resources required.

(4) *Execution*: The final phase is the implementation of the selected ideas through structured experiments. This involves setting up the experiment, collecting and analysing data, and then learning from the outcomes. The execution phase is where hypotheses are tested, and insights are gathered to inform future strategies. If the experiment fails, other previously shelved ideas are tested. In this phase it is key to select the proper metrics/KPIs assess the effectiveness of the strategy and to test the hypotheses.

This experimentation process enables businesses and organisations to systematically explore and validate growth strategies, ensuring that they are continually adapting and optimising their approaches based on empirical evidence.

To make it clear, let's see an example. Imagine an e-commerce clothing brand, which, after a comprehensive analysis of various factors, set up the objective of increasing the website conversion rate by 20% in the next quarter.

Phase 1: Ideation

The team brainstorms various ideas to improve the website's conversion rate. Ideas include:

(1) Implementing a chatbot to assist customers in their shopping journey.

(2) Offering a first-purchase discount for new email subscribers.

(3) Adding customer reviews and ratings on product pages.

(4) Creating bundle offers for related products at a discounted rate.

(5) Enhancing the website's mobile responsiveness.

Phase 2: Prioritisation (Using the ICE Method)

Each idea is evaluated using the ICE method:

(1) *Chatbot assistance:*
- Impact: 7 (could significantly improve customer service and engagement).
- Confidence: 5 (uncertain about the chatbot's effectiveness in increasing sales).
- Ease: 6 (requires moderate effort to implement).
- ICE score: 6.

(2) *First-purchase discount:*
- Impact: 8 (high likelihood of attracting new customers).
- Confidence: 8 (proven effectiveness in other businesses).
- Ease: 9 (easy to implement through email marketing tools).
- ICE Score: 8.3.

(3) *Customer reviews and ratings:*
- Impact: 9 (highly likely to build trust and influence purchase decisions).
- Confidence: 9 (backed by strong evidence from market research).
- Ease: 7 (requires time to collect and display reviews).
- ICE score: 8.3.

And so on for the other ideas.

Phase 3: Testing

Based on the ICE scores, the team decides to test the *customer reviews and ratings* feature first, as it has one of the highest scores and is expected to significantly influence conversion rates.

A/B testing is set up where half of the product pages show customer reviews and ratings, while the other half remains unchanged. The test runs for a specified period, and the conversion rates are closely monitored.

Phase 4: Analysis and Iteration

After the testing period:

- *If the experiment succeeds* (conversion rate increases significantly), the feature is implemented across all product pages, and the team moves on to test the next high-priority idea.

- *If the experiment fails,* the feature is refined based on feedback, or the team moves on to test the next idea, such as the *first-purchase discount.*

This process exemplifies a structured approach to growth hacking, where ideas are systematically generated, prioritised, tested, and iterated upon based on empirical data, ensuring continuous improvement and optimisation towards the set objective.

This process can also be implemented in contexts other than product development or customer experience. For instance, imagine a company facing issues with employee engagement and retention. The company decides to increase employee satisfaction rates. To this end, the human resource management department generates ideas. During the prioritisation phase, it is decided to test the idea of offering smart working one additional day per week. At the end of the reference period, KPIs are evaluated (e.g. a satisfaction survey administered to employees).

4.6. ORGANISING THE TEAM

The role of the Growth Hacker, as defined by Sean Ellis, emphasises a relentless pursuit of growth. Ryan Holiday (2014), a notable author in the field, describes the growth hacker as 'a professional who transcends traditional marketing's guesswork and instead embraces testable, trackable, and scalable methods'. This role is deeply focussed on data collection and analysis, recognising data as an increasingly vital resource. The importance of data in the modern world has elevated the growth hacker to one of the most sought-after professions, distinguished by a diverse array of skills that mark them as a multidisciplinary figure.

The growth hacker's training (see Fig. 7), often referred to as 'T-shaped', combines broad cross-cutting qualities (soft skills) and deep specialised competencies (hard skills). The horizontal bar of the 'T' represents a wide array of general soft skills, while the vertical bar symbolises deep, specialised hard skills. These skills, together with field experience, make the growth hacker a prominent figure in their sector.

When it comes to developing these skills, two primary methods are key: mastering the basics (Width of Knowledge) and delving deep (Depth of Knowledge). A solid foundation in diverse skills enables growth hackers to tackle complex problems effectively. They do not rely solely on traditional tools like ads or email marketing but on a range of pillars including data analysis, Lean start-up principles, understanding user psychology, and effective copywriting.

Further, the role requires continuous learning and specialisation. Growth hackers must avoid being jacks-of-all-trades but masters of none. Focussing on deepening specific areas of expertise is crucial for becoming an influential figure within an organisation.

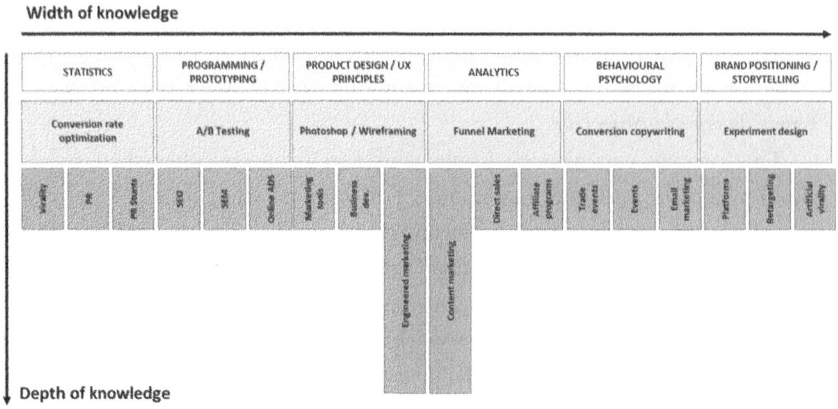

Fig. 7. The T-shaped Knowledge Capabilities of the Growth Hacker.
Source: Authors' elaboration.

Choosing the right projects is essential for skill development. The growth hacker should favour projects with significant impact on the company and its team, often finding value in complex and challenging tasks that drive organisational growth.

A growth hacker serves multiple roles:

- A facilitator, smoothing out conflicts and fostering experimentation.
- An idea generator, creating a fertile environment for creativity.
- A process manager.
- A data analyst, interpreting data to resolve bottlenecks.
- An advocate for growth in all forms, adapting to the organisational culture and business needs.

To sum up, the growth hacker acts as orchestrator of the team's efforts, responsible for setting growth objectives, coordinating experiments, and ensuring that the team's activities align with the overall business strategy. This person must possess a strong background in both marketing and analytics, coupled with leadership skills to guide and inspire the team.

4.6.1. The Growth Team

While a single growth hacker is vital for a company, especially start-ups, the collective effort of a cohesive, skilled team often surpasses individual achievements. Companies advancing to significant stages often establish a growth team. As Brian Balfour puts it, a growth team is a versatile, data-driven group, constantly seeking new strategies and tactics to test. This team comprises professionals from engineering, design, marketing, and analytics, working in fast-paced iterative cycles to boost growth rates.

The growth team's success lies in the diversity of its members' expertise. The team usually includes a growth master or Head of Growth, ensuring process adherence and effective information management. Alongside them are the full-stack developer, focussing on pragmatic product development; the UX designer, crafting an optimal customer journey; and the data analyst, who interprets vast data sets and communicates across different company functions. This compact but effective team typically consists of the growth master, developer, designer, marketer, and data analyst, each playing a crucial role in the team's success.

Larger companies, on the other hand, can organise the growth hacking team by taking human resources from different business functions, such as marketing, finance, product development, and so on. Therefore, ad hoc growth hacking teams can be formed to achieve specific goals or to follow specific projects.

Below are discussed some key roles that are important when managing growth strategies.

- *Data analyst*: the insights generator, tasked with collecting, analysing, and interpreting data from various experiments and marketing efforts. Their expertise helps the team make informed decisions, identify successful tactics, and pivot away from less effective strategies.

- *Product manager*: often working closely with the growth lead, the product manager ensures that the product development is tightly integrated with growth initiatives. They focus on improving user experience and product–market fit, essential for sustainable growth.

- *Content creator*: the voice of the team, creating compelling content that attracts, engages, and retains users. This role requires creativity, a deep understanding of the target audience, and the ability to craft messages that resonate across various channels.

- *Engineer and developer*: the technical powerhouse, capable of implementing the necessary tools, features, and integrations to support growth experiments. Their work enables the rapid deployment of testable ideas and the technical analysis of their performance.

- *Marketing specialist*: experts in SEO, SEM, social media, email marketing, and other channels; marketing specialists execute the campaigns designed to test hypotheses and drive growth. They are adept at adjusting strategies based on performance data and emerging trends.

The success of a growth hacking team hinges not just on the individual capabilities of its members but on their ability to work collaboratively in a fast-paced environment. This requires a culture that encourages experimentation, tolerates failure, and values learning from every outcome. Regular meetings to discuss results, share insights, and plan future experiments are vital for maintaining alignment and momentum. Knowledge sharing is key to making informed decisions and optimally navigating through the phases of growth, from problem identification to the testing of experiments. Without transparent sharing of all information, processes could be impacted by gaps, leading to poor effectiveness of growth strategies.

Equipping the team with the right tools for analytics, project management, communication, and automation is crucial for maintaining efficiency and effectiveness. Additionally, establishing processes that streamline experimentation – from hypothesis formation to testing and analysis – can significantly enhance the team's productivity.

Building and organising a growth hacking team is a strategic investment in the company's future. By assembling a group of talented individuals who bring together diverse skills and a shared commitment to growth, companies can navigate the complexities of the digital marketplace with greater agility and success. In doing so, they not only achieve their growth targets but also foster a culture of innovation and continuous learning.

We conclude by stating that the growth team is not always referred to by this name within companies. Some of the companies we interviewed (e.g. Utravel) entrust growth to the marketing department, which, however, works closely with other functions to increase the effectiveness of strategies.

5

GROWTH AND BUSINESS MODEL DYNAMICS

ABSTRACT

Scalability and optimisation/improvement are pivotal concepts in contemporary business landscapes, particularly in the realms of technology and online platforms. Scalability involves the capacity of a company or its processes to handle growth efficiently, often tied to economies of scale and cost advantages per unit. Optimisation/improvement, on the other hand, focusses on enhancing effectiveness and efficiency in resource utilisation and operational processes. This chapter delves into the intricacies of scalability and optimisation/improvement, drawing on real-world examples from companies such as Salesforce, Dropbox, and Airbnb. It explores how these companies leverage scalability to expand their operations and customer base while optimising processes to achieve better performance metrics. Furthermore, the chapter introduces case studies illustrating contrasting approaches to scalability and the challenges they face. Culminating in a comprehensive guide to determining the degree of scalability, the authors offer actionable steps for companies to assess their scalability potential. By analysing factors such as current resources, cost structure, market demand, and technological leverage, companies can align their growth hacking strategies with their scalability objectives effectively.

Keywords: Growth hacking; business model dynamics; scalability; optimisation; business model; growth orientation

5.1. ON SCALABILITY AND OPTIMISATION/IMPROVEMENT

Scalability is a fundamental concept in business and technology management, often associated with the ability of a company or its processes to handle growth effectively and efficiently (Giustiziero et al., 2022; Stampfl et al., 2013). It encompasses the capacity to expand operations, customer base, or infrastructure while maintaining or improving performance. Scalability is closely linked to the concept of 'economies of scale', where larger operations can often achieve cost advantages per unit, which can be a key driver of profitability (Acquier et al., 2019; Husan, 1997; Täuscher & Abdelkafi, 2018).

For example, consider a tech start-up that experiences rapid user growth for its mobile app. Scalability, in this context, involves ensuring that the app's infrastructure can handle the increased demand without a proportional increase in costs. Cloud-based services are commonly able to scale resources up or down based on user demand. For example, a cloud software company, such as Salesforce, achieves scalability by offering its CRM services to a growing number of businesses without needing to significantly change the core software for each new customer. Similarly, Dropbox is a classic example of using growth hacking to scale. They implemented a referral programme that rewarded existing users with additional storage space for every new user they brought in. This simple yet effective hack allowed Dropbox to rapidly increase its user base decreasing the customer acquisition costs (CAC). Airbnb optimised its listing visibility by cross-posting properties on Craigslist, which at the time had a larger user base. This not only improved the number of views for listings but also streamlined the process of attracting potential renters from outside their initial platform. Netflix scales its user base internationally by streaming content over the internet, bypassing the traditional physical distribution challenges of cable networks. LinkedIn scaled its professional network by encouraging new users to upload their entire email address book, which helped them to quickly and automatically connect with contacts who were already on the platform or invite new users.

It's quite easy to infer that, in general, platforms scale more easily compared to traditional businesses (Ronteau et al., 2022). For example, Amazon tends to earn more per customer with its Amazon Web Services (AWS) than with its retail services. AWS provides cloud computing and hosting solutions to businesses, and its higher profit margins significantly contribute to Amazon's overall revenue. In contrast, the retail sector operates with lower margins due to the competitive nature of the e-commerce market. However, this also stems from the scalability of the business. The fixed and marginal costs of the retail business are considerably higher compared to those related to the cloud business.

The main consequence of all this is that Amazon creates synergies between its various businesses. Investing in retail allows to increase the number of business customers and end-users. In this way, the American company can offer cloud services to a growing number of customers without proportionally increasing costs, thus scaling the AWS further.

Optimisation/improvement refers to the process of making the most effective or efficient use of available resources or systems (Varga et al., 2023). In a business context, it involves fine-tuning various aspects of operations, marketing efforts, or processes to improve performance metrics, such as conversion rates, user engagement, or cost reduction. Optimisation is driven by the quest for efficiency and the desire to maximise outcomes with minimal resources (Maiti et al., 2020). For example, a Software as a Service (SaaS) company might employ optimisation strategies to enhance its sales funnel. This could involve analysing user behaviour data to identify points of drop-off and then conducting A/B tests on landing pages to determine which design or messaging leads to higher conversion rates. Thus, optimisation aims to refine existing processes for better results. For instance, Nike optimises its supply chain management to reduce production costs and time to market. By employing just-in-time manufacturing and automation, Nike can efficiently manage inventory levels, reduce waste, and respond more quickly to market trends. Twitter optimised user engagement by introducing features like the 'What's happening' box and the use of hashtags, which encouraged users to post more frequently and engage with trending topics, thereby increasing the time spent on the platform and the number of interactions.

Optimisation can be also deemed an improvement process, like an ongoing and iterative process aimed at enhancing the effectiveness, efficiency, or performance of a business's operations, products, or services. Continuous improvement is a core principle of many successful organisations. For example, an e-commerce retailer may embark on a journey of improvement by addressing a customer pain point. For instance, they notice that slow shipping times are discouraging repeat customers. Through data analysis and growth hacking techniques, they identify bottlenecks in their logistics and distribution network. By optimising shipping processes, they significantly improve delivery times, leading to improved customer satisfaction and retention. IKEA, for example, continuously improves its product designs and customer service experience. They innovate by offering flat-packed furniture, which reduces shipping costs and storage space, and improves customer convenience. Uber improved its customer experience by implementing dynamic pricing, known as surge pricing. This algorithmic approach adjusted fares in real time based on rider demand and driver availability, which helped to balance supply and demand, and improve service reliability during peak times. Nike has used growth hacking strategies to improve its product offerings and marketing. By leveraging user data and engagement through their Nike+ community, they have been able to gather insights into consumer behaviour and preferences to drive product development and customer loyalty programmes.

In essence, scalability is about the capacity for growth, optimisation, and improvement focus on efficiency and effectiveness. While these concepts have distinct objectives, they are often interrelated. Growth hacking, with its data-driven and experimental approach, can be a valuable tool in achieving all three, as it enables businesses to adapt and evolve in response to changing circumstances and customer needs.

Hence, before developing growth strategies, it is vital to analyse the scalability potential of a company. In this context, as anticipated, scalability refers to the company's ability to handle a significant increase in workload, customers, or market demand without encountering a corresponding and proportionate increase in operational complexity or costs. Scalability is closely tied to the concept of how costs, both fixed and variable, scale with the growth of the business (Moro-Visconti et al., 2020; Rummel et al., 2022).

Fixed costs are costs that do not change with the level of output or sales. Examples include rent, salaries of permanent staff, or the cost of purchasing or maintaining equipment. In a scalable business model, fixed costs play a critical role. If a company can increase its output or sales while keeping these fixed costs constant, it achieves economies of scale. This means that as the company grows, the average cost per unit of output decreases, making the business more profitable as it scales. If this is the case, the company should try to scale as much as possible. For instance, a software company has high initial fixed costs (like development costs) but very low marginal costs for each additional user. Therefore, once the development is complete, adding new users doesn't significantly increase costs, making the business model highly scalable.

Scalability also involves how *variable costs* are managed. While fixed costs remain constant, variable costs increase with output. In a scalable business model, the increase in variable costs is ideally lower than the increase in revenue, maintaining or improving the profit margin. For example, an e-commerce company that relies on drop shipping might have variable costs related to shipping and handling per order. If this company can negotiate better shipping rates as it grows, it can scale more effectively, as the increase in sales will outpace the increase in variable costs.

As such, there are companies with a business model that is highly scalable, while others have a lesser scalable business model. Cloud service providers like AWS and Drive exemplify highly scalable business models. Their platform offers cloud computing resources over the internet, catering to a wide range of customers from start-ups to large enterprises. Scalability in cloud services hinges on virtual resources. AWS can add more customers without significantly increasing their fixed costs. The infrastructure, such as data centres, is already in place and can support a large number of users. The cost to AWS for serving each additional customer is relatively low compared to the revenue generated. Moreover, as they grow their customer base, they can achieve economies of scale, further decreasing the average cost. Hence, their growth strategies will be aiming at scaling the business as much as possible. Contrast this with a traditional furniture manufacturing company. This type of business is less scalable due to the nature of its production and distribution, and thus to the nature of its costs.

Manufacturing physical goods involves significant variable costs – materials, labour, shipping, and so on, that increase with production volume. While there are some economies of scale, these businesses often face a linear relationship between costs and output. Additionally, expanding production often requires substantial investments in physical infrastructure, like factories and machineries, which represents a significant fixed cost that doesn't scale as efficiently as digital products. These types of companies should thus use growth hacking to optimise and improve business processes.

Netflix, Uber, Spotify, Tinder, Revolut, WhatsApp, Dropbox, LinkedIn, Facebook, Deliveroo, and similar platforms are all examples of digital platforms that are generally considered scalable, but the degree and nature of their scalability can vary based on several factors, including their cost structure, business model, market dynamics, and regulatory environment. Most digital platforms have relatively high fixed costs (e.g. R&D) and relatively low or zero variable and marginal costs. Hence, they need to scale a lot to create value.

The above-mentioned platforms present some similarities in their scalability trajectories, for example:

- *Low marginal cost of additional users*: These platforms typically have low marginal costs for adding additional users. For instance, adding a new user to Facebook or WhatsApp doesn't significantly increase the platform's operational costs.

- *Network effects*: Many of these platforms benefit from network effects. The more users they have, the more valuable the platform becomes for each user, which in turn attracts more users and complementors. LinkedIn's value, for example, increases as more professionals join and contribute to the network.

- *Digital nature*: Being digital platforms, they don't face the same physical constraints as traditional businesses. For example, Dropbox can scale its user base without needing to physically expand its infrastructure in the same way a traditional storage company would.

However, they also present some differences in scalability paths:

- *Content costs*: Platforms like Netflix and Spotify face significant costs related to content acquisition and production, which can impact their scalability. As they grow, they may need to invest more in content to keep attracting and retaining users, which can increase their costs considerably. Therefore, data analysis is critical for these companies to optimally manage the trade-off between content production/acquisition and quality of supply to customers.

- *Regulatory and operational challenges*: Platforms like Uber and Deliveroo operate in highly regulated spaces and face operational challenges (like managing a workforce of drivers) that can impact their scalability in different markets. In a similar vein, Revolut's scalability is partly dependent on its ability to navigate financial regulations in different countries, which can be a complex and costly process.

In summary, whether a business model is scalable or not depends on how well it can grow revenue while controlling or minimally increasing both fixed and variable costs. Scalable business models are particularly sought after, especially in technology and online sectors, where the ability to grow quickly and efficiently is a significant competitive advantage.

Young Platform (https://youngplatform.com/) is a crypto exchange that also offers education on cryptocurrencies in the form of training for those registered on the platform. After a phase of exponential growth with a strong focus on lead generation, the management witnessed a period of decline, influenced by socio-political crises, inflation, and economic downturns, leading to reduced investments. This prompted a reassessment of business strategies, with a heightened focus on retention. Reduced marketing investments led to a revisitation of business objectives and consequently, growth strategies. As suggested by one of the founders, once the platform reached two million subscribers, it had scaled sufficiently to shift focus towards retention. This led to the development of new products like Crypto Exchange-traded funds (ETFs), which should lead to increased loyalty, greater lifetime value (LTV), and better retention. This case demonstrates that growth is also essential for understanding and defining the most effective objectives for the organisation, which can be related to retention rather than acquisition, and generating corresponding strategies.

5.2. NOT ALL PLATFORMS ARE SCALABLE IN THE SAME WAY. THE CASE OF UTRAVEL

As platforms generally offer greater scalability than traditional business models, it's critical to acknowledge that not all platforms operate identically.

For instance, Utravel, an innovative start-up based in Turin and born as a spin-off of the Alpitour Group, made a unique pivot towards a scalable business model. Initially, Utravel launched the 'blind' model, targeting university students under 30 with the allure of discounted, mystery destinations. This model hinged on the availability of Alpitour's accommodation, making scalability a challenge due to its dependency on unsold rooms. Recognising the limitations of this approach, Utravel ventured into a more scalable and innovative model, the Naoclub.

The Naoclub model diverges significantly from traditional travel offerings, focussing on long-term rental of facilities and the organisation of trips led by local guides, known as Coach Travel. These coaches, deeply rooted in the destination's culture, offer travellers unique and authentic experiences. This model not only enhances the travel experience but also fosters a positive impact on local communities and cultures by creating employment opportunities and promoting sustainable tourism practices. Utravel's pivot reflects a strategic move towards creating a self-sustaining ecosystem that benefits all stakeholders, including travellers, local communities, and the company itself. By leveraging technology through a proprietary app, Utravel enhances customer experience by enabling users to book recommended experiences and access various services easily.

The shift towards the Naoclub model exemplifies Utravel's commitment to innovation, community engagement, and sustainability. It represents a harmonious blend of adventure, cultural immersion, and social interaction, all facilitated by a platform that values both the traveller's experience and the local community's well-being. This approach not only addresses the scalability concerns associated with the 'blind' model but also aligns with modern travellers' desires for more meaningful and impactful travel experiences.

In this sense, growth hacking plays a crucial role in optimising and enhancing this scalable model by employing creative marketing strategies, data analytics, and technology. By analysing traveller feedback and preferences, Utravel can continuously refine its offerings, ensuring a personalised and engaging customer journey. Moreover, the company can leverage growth hacking techniques to streamline operations, enhance user experience on the platform, and foster community growth through targeted engagement and content strategies.

In essence, Utravel's transition from the 'blind' model to the Naoclub represents a strategic evolution towards a more scalable, impactful, and user-centred platform. It underscores the potential of growth hacking not just for scalability but for fostering a vibrant community of travellers eager to explore the world in a more connected, sustainable, and meaningful way.

Despite this, the Naoclub too has some scalability limits, as discussed below.

- *Physical service delivery*: Utravel's offering involves organising and managing tangible travel experiences, inherently limiting scalability when compared to purely digital platforms. Each organised trip demands logistical planning, facility bookings, and coordination, challenging to scale with the same efficiency as digital services. In other terms, a limited number of travellers can access and enjoy each facility. In addition, it would be complex for Utravel to scale the number of destinations and the number of accommodation facilities in short time.

- *Quality control and personalisation*: As Utravel expands its number of trips and destinations, maintaining high-quality experiences and a personalised touch becomes increasingly difficult. In the travel industry, where customer satisfaction is paramount, this is especially crucial.

- *Resource intensiveness*: Scaling the model necessitates a significant increase in human resources for trip planning, management, and local guides, leading to potentially higher operational costs per trip and the complexities of managing travel logistics in diverse locations.

- *Regulatory and market variations*: Expanding into new geographical areas introduces the challenge of navigating varying travel regulations and market conditions, requiring a deep understanding and adaptation to these local nuances, which can be resource-intensive and complex.

Despite these limitations, the platform can leverage on various factors to boost scalability, among which:

- *Community and network effects*: By building a strong community of travellers and local guides, Utravel can leverage network effects. Satisfied customers and engaged local guides can recommend the platform to others, enhancing its appeal and potentially driving exponential growth.

- *Technology leverage*: Utilising digital tools for marketing, customer engagement, and operational management can significantly boost scalability. An online platform for booking, customer service, and community engagement can efficiently manage a larger volume of customers and improve the overall customer experience.

In essence, while Utravel operates on a business model that demonstrates potential scalability, the nature of its service – rooted in tangible travel experiences – presents unique challenges in scaling compared to purely digital platforms. The scalability of Utravel depends on effectively managing the resource-intensive aspects of travel organisations and adapting to the varied market conditions across different regions.

Approaching growth hacking with specific objectives is a strategic method to drive a company's growth, as outlined in the previous discussion on Utravel. This approach involves setting clear, measurable goals and deploying targeted strategies to achieve them. For Utravel, this means validating its various business models (such as the Blind, Naoclub, and Short Naoclub options) by filling rooms, enhancing traveller experiences to encourage positive word-of-mouth, engaging users to increase retention rates, and identifying new business opportunities through service development and geographic expansion. Table 4 shows and discusses some examples.

Table 4. Bridging Growth Hacking Goals and Strategies in Utravel.

Goal	Strategies	Explanation
Improving retention rates	Personalised communication	Analyse past trip data to understand customer preferences and tailor communication and trip suggestions accordingly. Personalised emails or notifications about upcoming trips aligned with their interests can increase repeat bookings
	Exclusive offers for repeat travellers	Offering incentives or exclusive deals to repeat customers can enhance loyalty. This could include discounts, early access to new trips, or special amenities
	Community engagement	Developing a robust online community platform where travellers can share stories, leave reviews, and interact can increase engagement and build a loyal customer base
	Feedback loops	Regularly gathering and analysing customer feedback can lead to improvements in trip offerings, customer service, and overall experience
Price optimisation (Dynamic Pricing)	Data-driven pricing strategies	Employ data analytics to implement dynamic pricing models. By analysing demand trends, booking patterns, and customer price sensitivity, they can adjust prices in real time to optimise revenue and occupancy rates
	A/B testing	Testing different price points for similar trips can provide insights into the price elasticity of their offerings, helping to determine the most effective pricing strategy

(Continued)

Table 4. Bridging Growth Hacking Goals and Strategies in Utravel (Continued)

Goal	Strategies	Explanation
Improving the website user experience	Website optimisation	Growth hacking can be used to continually test and optimise the website's layout, content, and user flow. Techniques like A/B testing or heat mapping can identify areas where users may be experiencing friction
	Enhancing search and recommendation algorithms	Implementing smarter search functionality and recommendation algorithms on the website can make it easier for users to find trips that interest them, improving engagement and potentially leading to higher conversion rates

Source: Authors' elaboration.

5.3. DETERMINING THE DEGREE OF SCALABILITY

Determining the degree of scalability of a business is a crucial step for a company before defining in growth hacking strategies. This helps the company to align its growth hacking efforts with its potential to scale, thus also driving resources allocation, strategy formulation, and team management.

> **Callout 13. Some Useful Steps to Analyse the Scalability of the Company.**
>
> - *Assess current resources and capabilities*:
>   - *Infrastructure*: Evaluate if the current infrastructure can handle increased demand. For digital companies, this might involve server capacity and technology stack. For physical goods or services, it involves production capacity and supply chain logistics.
>   - *Human resources*: Determine if the current team can manage increased workload or if scaling will require significant additional hiring.
> - *Understand cost structure*:
>   - *Analyse the fixed and variable costs* and how they will change with increased production or service provision. If costs rise steeply with increased output, scalability may be limited.
>   - *Calculate the marginal cost* of acquiring and serving one additional customer. Lower marginal costs typically indicate higher scalability.

- *Market demand and size*:
  - *Assess the market size and growth potential*. Even if a business is scalable in theory, limited market demand can constrain real-world scalability.
  - *Conduct market research* to understand potential demand at a larger scale.
- *Evaluate the business model*:
  - *Examine the business model* for scalability potential. Subscription models, SaaS, and platforms often have higher scalability compared to traditional retail or service businesses.
  - Consider the potential for *network effects*, where the value of a product or service increases as more people use it.
- *Regulatory and geographical constraints*:
  - *Identify any regulatory barriers* that might limit scaling, especially in highly regulated industries or when considering international expansion.
  - *Assess geographical constraints* and the ability to expand into new markets.
- *Technological leverage*:
  - *Evaluate how technology* can be used to scale operations, such as through automation, AI, and cloud computing.
  - *Consider the adaptability* of the technology stack to increased demand.
- *Financial health and funding*:
  - *Analyse the company's financial health* to determine if it can sustain growth. Consider cash flow, profit margins, and capital for investment.
  - *Assess funding options* for scaling, including venture capital, loans, or reinvesting profits.

- *Historical Data and Trends*:
  - *Look at historical growth patterns* and how the company has managed past scaling challenges.
  - *Analyse CAC and LTV* over time to understand scalability trends. If CAC is low and LTV potentially high, there is a higher chance of sustainable scaling
- *Competitive analysis*:
  - *Understand the competitive landscape* and how competitors have scaled. This can provide insights into potential challenges and opportunities.

Numerous contemporary triumphs among rapidly expanding companies, such as Facebook, Groupon, and Salesforce.com, trace their roots back to internet start-ups that evolved into multi-million-dollar enterprises. Over the past 15 years, the internet has emerged as a pivotal technological force, fostering a fertile ground for innovative business models. Given the affordability of experimenting with diverse business models, these start-ups frequently undergo multiple revisions before achieving profitability. Consequently, the internet serves as an exceptionally rich empirical backdrop for studying successful business model innovations (Wirtz et al., 2010). By conducting a thorough analysis of these factors, a company can gauge its scalability and tailor its growth hacking strategies to effectively utilise its resources, capitalise on market opportunities, and overcome potential scaling challenges.

6

FACTORS DRIVING GROWTH

ABSTRACT

Product-led growth (PLG) represents a paradigm shift in business strategy, prioritising the product itself as the primary driver of growth rather than relying heavily on traditional sales and marketing methods. In this framework, companies focus on creating exceptional products that directly address user needs, delivering optimised user experiences, fostering virality through word-of-mouth endorsements, and simplifying access and onboarding processes. This approach capitalises on identifying underserved markets or unmet needs, often requiring in-depth market research and education efforts. This chapter explores various growth factors beyond PLG, including community-led, content-led, ecosystem-led, brand-led, service-led, price-led, acquisition-led, regulatory-led, investor-led, and velocity-driven growth strategies. Case studies of successful companies such as Slack, Zoom, Dropbox, Treedom, Facebook (Meta), BlaBlaCar, Spotify, Revolut, and others illustrate the efficacy of these growth strategies in diverse industries. Additionally, the concept of velocity-driven growth, emphasising rapid scale and market dominance, highlights the importance of speed and agility in competitive markets. Ultimately, effective scaling requires a multifaceted approach, often combining several growth factors tailored to the company's unique circumstances and market dynamics. Flexibility and continuous experimentation are essential, allowing companies to adapt their growth strategies to evolving market conditions and emerging opportunities.

Keywords: Growth hacking; growth drivers; ecosystem; rapid experimentation; scalability; firm growth

The term *product-led growth (PLG)* denotes a strategic approach that positions the product as the pivotal element in a company's growth trajectory. Rather than predominantly depending on conventional sales and marketing for expansion, enterprises embracing a PLG framework concentrate on:

- *Developing an outstanding product* that efficiently addresses a user's problem or meets a specific need.
- *Delivering an optimised user experience* that promotes the adoption and utilisation of the product by newcomers.
- Fostering *virality and organic growth* through word-of-mouth endorsements from current users.
- *Simplifying access and the onboarding process*, often via complimentary versions or trial periods, enabling users to discern the product's value prior to committing to a purchase.

This methodology stands in stark contrast to traditional paradigms, which heavily lean on sales and marketing divisions to cultivate leads and finalise transactions. With PLG, the product itself takes the lead in attracting, converting, and retaining customers.

In this scenario, growth stems from identifying a market segment that is either underserved or has an unmet need not yet fulfilled by existing companies. This strategy involves in-depth market research and targeting. In some cases, companies meet a demand already served but through a different business model, which can bring more benefits to the consumer. For example, Spotify revolutionised the music industry by offering a platform to listen to millions of different songs on repeat and at any time, without having to purchase CDs or vinyl records. Hence, the potential market is a key variable in the scalability of the business. Companies implementing business models in large markets are more likely to achieve high growth rates. Another important factor in developing this growth model is education because often these models are new compared to the past, and the consumer needs to familiarise themselves with the new solution. Dropbox, in its early days, shared videos to explain how its cloud service worked. Market education, thus, can both inhibit and support business model scalability. In uneducated markets, where prospective customers don't comprehend the product or service's utility, entering becomes challenging. Investing in customer education, that is, explaining the product or service before selling it, hampers scalability. Yet, once target customers are familiar with the offering, business expansion becomes easier. Market education can be advantageous for fast followers, as the initial company paves the way for others by familiarising customers with a new business idea.

This approach starkly diverges from conventional strategies that are predominantly dependent on sales and marketing teams for lead generation and sales closure. In contrast, within the PLG framework, the product itself emerges as the foremost catalyst for customer acquisition, conversion, and expansion.

Treedom is an innovative platform that allows individuals and companies to plant trees and follow their growth online, contributing to environmental sustainability and social development projects around the world. The platform connects people with farmers, creating a direct link between the action of planting a tree and its long-term growth and benefits, such as CO_2 absorption, biodiversity enhancement, and providing economic opportunities to agricultural communities. Given its business model and how it operates, Treedom could be considered a case of PLG, albeit in a slightly unconventional sense compared to technology or software companies typically associated with PLG. While Treedom's approach incorporates the foundational elements of PLG, it also highlights the versatility of the PLG model beyond its traditional tech-centric domain. Treedom leverages its product (in this case, the planting and tracking of trees) to drive growth, user acquisition, and expansion, aligning well with the essence of PLG strategies.

Key advantages of PLG encompass:

- Decreased customer acquisition costs (CAC), as the product inherently generates interest and draws in users, eliminating the necessity for substantial investments in marketing and sales efforts.

- Enhanced user retention and lifetime value (LTV), attributed to the significant focus on user experience and the superior quality of the product.

- Facilitated scalability, given that the product naturally supports organic growth and market penetration.

Noteworthy instances of companies that have efficaciously implemented a PLG strategy include renowned names like Slack, Zoom, and Dropbox, among others. These examples highlight the power of a product-centric approach in catalysing remarkable growth.

The second factor is *the role of communities and virality (community- and network-led growth)*. The concept of 'network externalities' or 'network effects' (Shapiro & Varian, 2010) has been extensively explored in various studies, offering both theoretical and empirical support for its strategic significance. Positive network effects occur when consumers value a product more as more people use it (Gregory et al., 2021). Such effects are considered determinants of product success when they positively impact a product's economic value

(Gregory et al., 2021). Social networks, exemplified by Facebook, showcase this phenomenon. Facebook's value as a social network platform grows with each user, as users invite friends and share the platform. However, network effects can act as a scalability factor, shifting from a positive supporting effect to a negative inhibiting one, or vice versa. Research indicates a positive relationship between the size of internet communities and business model scalability. Larger communities facilitate more transactions, leading to increased margins and transaction-based revenues for the website operator. However, formerly positive network externalities can turn negative as the network exceeds a specific size, as observed in peer-to-peer music sharing networks (Asvanund et al., 2004). In designing business models where the size of the user base affects consumer 'tastes', scalability considerations should encompass critical mass and going viral. Critical mass, defined by Markus (1987), suggests that once a critical number of users are attracted, the use of an interactive medium should spread rapidly throughout the community. This concept is particularly crucial for community-based business models (e.g. Instagram, TikTok) (Bargoni et al., 2024). Achieving critical mass is often essential for viable revenue sources like advertising and transaction commissions. Employing viral marketing techniques to reach critical mass and foster positive network externalities is a key element for scalability in this type of growth. Going viral, integrated into the business model, can expedite scaling by leveraging brand evangelists and quickly raising awareness for new offerings. As analysed in Chapter 2, it is crucial in the context of platforms to understand whether the business model is subject to direct and/or indirect network effects. This analysis will guide growth strategies. For example, in the context of platforms like Satispay, Splitwise, and Revolut, referral programmes are very effective precisely because these are platforms with strong direct network effects.

The third factor is *content-led growth*, which means leveraging high-quality, unique, or user-generated content as the main draw for users. This strategy relies on the value of the content to attract and retain users. For example, YouTube has scaled massively by providing a platform for user-generated video content, attracting millions of content creators and viewers. Similarly, Twitch began as a platform primarily for gaming content and expanded significantly as content creators and viewers joined the platform for its live-streaming content. In this context, platform leaders aim to share content that may interest users, exploiting virality and network effects.

The fourth factor is *ecosystem-led growth*, or creating a network of complementary products, services, or users that become more valuable as additional participants join. This interdependence often leads to a more robust and stickier platform. Google has built an extensive ecosystem with its suite of interconnected products (like Gmail, Google Drive, and Google Maps), enhancing the overall value of its platform. Successful companies like Apple and Microsoft leverage the strength of external developers to offer their users ever-improving apps. ChatGPT, with its premium version, has opened its business model to allow the integration of many software applications that can add value to its value proposition. As suggested by Cusumano et al. (2019), platforms can be transactional or innovation. Innovation platforms specifically are built on the ability to attract complementors capable of developing innovative applications.

The fifth factor is *brand-led growth*, which means establishing a strong brand identity and emotional connection with users. This strategy typically involves significant investment in marketing and brand experience. Disney+ has been able to enter the streaming service industry thanks to its powerful and well-known brand along with the offering of well-known movies produced internally. Therefore, it is reasonable to infer that this strategy is much more effective if used by companies that already possess a strong brand and decide to enter new businesses related to the platform world. The brand often serves as a guarantee of quality, relevant content, and long-term vision.

The sixth factor is *service-led growth*, which implies differentiating the platform through superior customer service and user support, ensuring high satisfaction, and encouraging positive word-of-mouth referrals. This factor refers to growth strategies that come after the validation and adoption of the platform. It is often associated with a moment when competition is won thanks to additional services that can somehow represent a source of competitive advantage. For example, Netflix provides a high-quality, on-demand streaming service with a focus on customer experience, including personalised recommendations and a vast content library. Use customer feedback loops to refine service offerings and implement features that increase convenience, such as easy sign-up processes or responsive customer support. Duolingo utilises content-led growth by offering a broad range of language courses that are accessible and entertaining, drawing users through the quality and diversity of its educational content. The platform also employs elements of Gamification, which, while not a category I previously listed, is a powerful engagement tool that encourages regular use and retention. Users are motivated to continue their language learning through in-app rewards, streaks, and a competitive points system. Hence, this factor also involves the introduction of novel features, technologies, or business models that keep the platform at the cutting edge and attractive to users who seek the latest innovations. This factor can intersect with other factors, creating a mutually supportive mechanism. Consider, for example, Sony PlayStation, which develops new versions of its consoles, motivating the development of games by software developers (ecosystem-led growth and indirect network effects).

The seventh factor is *price-led growth*. In this case, competition shifts to price, with a focus on reducing costs compared to competitors. This context also represents a more advanced phase in the product or service lifecycle. This can be achieved through efficiencies, economies of scale, or a low-price, high-volume business model. Spotify has been able to scale in the competitive music streaming market by offering a freemium model that provides a free ad-supported service alongside premium subscriptions. This example shows that price convenience is not only relative to competitors but also compared to alternative technologies, such as CDs and vinyl in the case of Spotify and streaming in general. The e-commerce platform Temu is scaling globally thanks to very competitive prices on a wide range of products. Known for its low-priced goods ranging from electronics to clothing, Wish connects customers directly to manufacturers, eliminating the middlemen and offering products at significantly reduced prices. Specialising in fashion and accessories, Shein has gained a massive following by offering trendy items at low prices. The company leverages data analytics to identify fashion trends and manage its supply chain efficiently, enabling rapid production of popular items.

The eighth factor is linked to the acquisition of other companies (*acquisition-led growth*). A prime example is Facebook (Meta), which has grown its platform through the acquisitions of Instagram, WhatsApp, and Oculus, among others, expanding its user base and product offerings. As seen in Chapter 2, platforms can grow thanks to economies of scope, finding synergies between various businesses when they manage to scale the initial services offered. BlaBlaCar, a leading carpooling platform that connects drivers with empty seats to passengers looking for a ride over long distances, has effectively used acquisitions as part of its growth and scaling strategy. By acquiring similar companies around the world, BlaBlaCar has been able to quickly expand its geographical footprint and user base, leveraging existing platforms to enter new markets with ease. Examples of BlaBlaCar's acquisition strategy include the purchase of Carpooling.com and AutoHop, two major European carpooling platforms, which significantly boosted its presence in Europe.

The ninth factor is *regulatory-led growth*, which implies utilising changes in regulation or designing the platform to comply with or benefit from existing regulations, creating a competitive advantage or market opportunity.

The process of designing a scalable business model must incorporate awareness of legal constraints. A notable example is the Swedish company Spotify, which faced challenges related to differing intellectual property rights systems in various countries, demonstrating the importance of adapting to diverse legal frameworks to facilitate geographical expansion and internationalisation, as seen in services like Dropbox. Another example is Revolut, which has benefitted from regulatory environments that support innovation in financial services. For instance, in Europe, the Revised Payment Services Directive (PSD2) has opened up the banking industry to non-banks and fintech companies by requiring banks to provide access to their customer data (with the customer's consent) to third-party providers. This regulation has allowed Revolut to offer a range of financial services, such as budgeting, currency exchange without bank fees, and stock trading, by leveraging access to banking data and infrastructure. Revolut's ability to navigate and take advantage of such regulatory frameworks has been a key factor in its rapid growth and expansion across Europe and beyond.

The 10th factor is *investor-led growth*. While a company's growth positively affects investor attractiveness, the reverse relationship also holds true. New ventures with scalable business models are more likely to attract external funding, leading to accelerated company growth, as suggested by entrepreneurship theory. Similarly, in 'Blitzscaling', the authors, Reid Hoffman and Chris Yeh, emphasise that the growth trajectory of a start-up can be significantly influenced by the quality of its investors and the talent it attracts. The Silicon Valley ecosystem is highlighted as a prime example of a conducive environment for rapid start-up growth, partly due to the abundance of experienced venture capitalists (VCs) and a dense concentration of talent. The region is renowned for its network of seasoned investors who not only provide capital but also strategic guidance, industry connections, and mentorship. These investors often have a keen understanding of the tech landscape, market dynamics, and the challenges of scaling rapidly. By contrast, while New York and other tech hubs also have vibrant start-up ecosystems with access to venture capital, Silicon Valley's historical depth in tech investments and its culture of risk-taking can offer start-ups a unique advantage in terms of the breadth and depth of investment expertise. Moreover, Silicon Valley's culture is more tolerant of risk and failure, encouraging ambitious projects and experimentation. This attitude can attract both investors and talents who are eager to push boundaries and innovate, further fuelling the rapid growth of start-ups.

The last factor, called *velocity-driven growth,* refers to a strategic approach that prioritises rapid scale and market dominance over initial efficiency or profitability. This concept, deeply rooted in the principles of 'Blitzscaling' as outlined by Reid Hoffman and Chris Yeh (2018), emphasises the critical importance of speed in achieving and sustaining a competitive advantage in fast-evolving markets. Velocity-driven growth is characterised by aggressive investment in scaling operations, product development, and market expansion with the goal of capturing market share and establishing network effects before competitors. This strategy often involves making calculated high-risk decisions under conditions of uncertainty, with the understanding that the first mover or the fastest scaler can secure a disproportionately large share of the market value. Key components of velocity-driven growth include:

- *Rapid experimentation and iteration*: Quickly testing and refining products to meet market demands and user needs, even if it means foregoing short-term efficiency.

- *Aggressive resource allocation*: Investing significant resources into growth, often supported by substantial venture capital, to fuel expansion efforts and scale operations quickly.

- *Focus on market leadership*: The ultimate goal is to become the dominant player in the market, under the belief that the market leader enjoys significant advantages in terms of brand recognition, customer loyalty, and economies of scale.

While velocity-driven growth can lead to massive success, as evidenced by companies like Amazon, Netflix, and LinkedIn, it also comes with high risks. The strategy requires a delicate balance between speed and sustainability, demanding continuous adaptation and a keen sense of when to pivot or double down on growth tactics. In its early days, Airbnb faced stiff competition from Wimdu, a German company that was essentially a clone of Airbnb and had substantial financial backing from Rocket Internet, a company known for quickly launching copycats of successful American tech start-ups in other markets. Wimdu was well funded, receiving around $90 million in investment to aggressively expand in the global market and compete directly with Airbnb. The situation posed a significant threat to Airbnb, which at the time was still trying to establish itself as a global leader in the emerging market of online accommodation sharing. Despite the challenge, Airbnb chose to engage in a battle for market dominance by raising significant capital and boosting a rapid global expansion. In fact, Airbnb aggressively expanded its presence worldwide, focussing on improving its service, user experience, and establishing a strong brand in a short timeframe. Entering for first in various geographical markets led Airbnb to a significant first-mover advantage. A breakdown of this is displayed in Table 5.

Table 5. Growth Driving Factors and Implications for Growth Hacking.

Type	Definition	Literature Sources	Example	Implications for Growth Hacking
Product-led growth	The term *product-led growth (PLG)* denotes a strategic approach that positions the product as the pivotal element in a company's growth trajectory. Rather than predominantly depending on conventional sales and marketing for expansion, enterprises embracing a PLG framework concentrate on: Developing an outstanding product; delivering an optimised user experience; fostering virality and organic growth through word-of-mouth endorsements from current users; simplifying access and the onboarding process, often via complimentary versions or trial periods. Finally it involves focussing on identifying and serving a specific market segment that is underserved or has unmet needs	Zott et al. (2011)	Deliveroo – Started as a small start-up addressing the high-demand market for food delivery from quality restaurants that didn't traditionally offer delivery Canva – Identified a market for easy-to-use graphic design tools, filling the gap between complex professional software and basic design tools Treedom is an innovative platform that allows individuals and companies to plant trees and follow their growth online, contributing to environmental sustainability and social development projects around the world. Scalapay identified a demand in the market for flexible payment solutions. By offering BNPL services, they cater to consumers looking for alternative financing options that do not require traditional credit checks or incur interest charges	Focus on market segmentation and targeted marketing. Offer tailored solutions or promotions to different customer segments. *Amazon*
Community and network-led growth	Building and nurturing a community around the platform to foster engagement, loyalty, and organic growth through word-of-mouth and peer-to-peer interactions. Leveraging on network effects	Kohler et al. (2011)	Fishbrain – A niche app for anglers to share catches and fishing spots, building a dedicated community around a shared hobby	Use virality. Encourage current users to invite others. Freemium models or free periods can be effective in quickly building a user base. *WhatsApp*

(Continued)

Table 5. Growth Driving Factors and Implications for Growth Hacking. (Continued)

Type	Definition	Literature Sources	Example	Implications for Growth Hacking
			Stack Overflow – Grew by fostering a community of developers helping each other solve coding problems, becoming the go-to platform for coding queries	Engage with core users and build features that encourage community interaction and contribution, such as forums, shared projects, or collaborative tools. *GitHub*
			LinkedIn has grown by leveraging professional networking, building a community where professionals come to connect, share insights, and find career opportunities	
			Uber benefits from indirect network effects, as more drivers and riders join the platform	
			Revolut and Splitwise users perceive higher value when an additional user adopts the platform. This because that user can interact with more users	
Content-led Growth	Leveraging high-quality, unique, or user-generated content as the main draw for users. This strategy relies on the value of the content to attract and retain users	Kapoor and Agarwal (2017)	YouTube has scaled massively by providing a platform for user-generated video content, attracting millions of content creators and viewers	Leverage user-generated content to create a self-sustaining cycle of content creation and consumption. Use algorithms to promote high-engagement content. *YouTube*
			Acast – A platform that supports podcast creators with hosting, distribution, and monetisation, growing as more quality content creators join	
			Twitch – Started as a platform primarily for gaming content and expanded significantly as content creators and viewers joined the platform for its live-streaming content	

Ecosystem-led Growth	Creating a network of complementary products, services, or users that become more valuable as additional participants join. This interdependence often leads to a more robust and sticky platform	Adner (2017)	Google has built an extensive ecosystem with its suite of interconnected products (like Gmail, Google Drive, and Google Maps), enhancing the overall value of its platform Zapier – Offers integrations between web apps, allowing users to automate workflows, creating an ecosystem of app connectivity Slack – Expanded from a messaging app to a collaboration hub with integrations and apps, creating an extensive ecosystem for work Microsoft has exhibited Ecosystem-led Growth through its integrated suite of software products and services, encouraging users to stay within the Microsoft ecosystem	Develop APIs and encourage third-party developers to create complementary apps or services that enhance the core platform's value. *Google Android*.
Brand-led Growth	Establishing a strong brand identity and emotional connection with users. This strategy typically involves significant investment in marketing and brand experience	Keller (2013)	Apple's success with its App Store can be attributed to its strong brand, which emphasises design, quality, and a seamless user experience Warby Parker – Initially an online platform for trying and buying eyewear, it built a strong brand around affordability and customer experience Peloton – Created a fitness community around its brand, leveraging high-quality content and interactive experiences to grow its platform Disney+ has been able to enter the streaming service industry thanks to the powerful and well know brand along with the offering of well-known movies internally produced	Invest in brand storytelling and user experience. Create a strong brand image that users want to be associated with. *Apple*

(*Continued*)

Table 5. Growth Driving Factors and Implications for Growth Hacking. *(Continued)*

Type	Definition	Literature Sources	Example	Implications for Growth Hacking
Innovation and Service-led Growth	Differentiating the platform through superior customer service and user support, ensuring high satisfaction and encouraging positive word-of-mouth referrals	Cusumano et al. (2019)	Duolingo utilises Content-led Growth by offering a broad range of language courses that are accessible and entertaining, drawing users through the quality and diversity of its educational content. The platform also employs elements of Gamification, which, while not a category I previously listed, is a powerful engagement tool that encourages regular use and retention. Users are motivated to continue their language learning through in-app rewards, streaks, and a competitive points system	Use customer feedback loops to refine service offerings. Implement features that increase convenience, such as easy sign-up processes or responsive customer support. Introduce new features to boost retention and referral. *Duolingo*
	Also, continuously introducing novel features, technologies, or business models that keep the platform at the cutting edge and attractive to users who seek the latest innovations	Ostrom et al. (2010)	Square – Expanded by continually innovating with new financial products and services for small businesses and individuals Netflix provides a high-quality, on-demand streaming service with a focus on customer experience, including personalised recommendations and a vast content library Calendly – Simplifies scheduling without the back-and-forth emails, growing rapidly due to its superior service and user experience DocuSign – Grew by providing a service that simplifies the process of electronic agreements and signatures, a vital service in many industries	Continuously release cutting-edge features that users are excited to try, share, and talk about. *OpenAI*

Price-led Growth	Competing on price by offering lower costs than competitors. This can be achieved through efficiencies, economies of scale, or a low-price, high-volume business model	Nagle and Hogan (2006)	Spotify has been able to scale in the competitive music streaming market by offering a freemium model that provides a free ad-supported service alongside premium subscriptions FreedomPop – Offered free mobile phone and wireless internet service, disrupting the market with its pricing model and growing its user base Robinhood – Initially grew its platform by offering commission-free trading, which was a game-changer in terms of pricing in the brokerage industry Temu is scaling globally thanks to very competitive prices on a wide range of products	Offer a freemium model where basic services are free, and premium features are behind a paywall. Use pricing tiers to capture a larger segment of the market. *Spotify*
Acquisition-led Growth	Growing the user base and capabilities of the platform through the acquisition of other companies, technologies, or teams	Graebner et al. (2010)	PillPack – Started as a medication delivery service and scaled up until it was acquired by Amazon, which expanded its reach GitHub – Grew by acquiring other developer tools and expanding its features, before being acquired by Microsoft, which further accelerated its growth Facebook (Meta) has grown its platform through the acquisitions of Instagram, WhatsApp, and Oculus, among others, expanding its user base and product offerings Microsoft has a history of Acquisition-led Growth, incorporating a range of software solutions and platforms into its business BlaBlaCar scaled its business model by acquiring similar companies all over the world	Look for strategic partnerships or acquisitions that can add new user segments, technologies, or capabilities to the existing platform. *Facebook*

(Continued)

Table 5. Growth Driving Factors and Implications for Growth Hacking. (Continued)

Type	Definition	Literature Sources	Example	Implications for Growth Hacking
Regulatory-led Growth	Exploiting changes in regulation or designing the platform to comply with or benefit from existing regulations, which can create a competitive advantage or market opportunity	David and Greenstein (1990)	Betterment – Leveraged changing regulations around financial advice to provide robo-advisor services, tapping into a new market segment Coinbase – Grew by navigating the complex regulatory landscape of cryptocurrencies, becoming one of the leading platforms for buying and trading digital assets PayPal grew by navigating the regulatory landscape of online payments, establishing trust and security in digital financial transactions	Focus on compliance and security as a key selling point. Use regulatory changes as opportunities to capture new markets or create trust. *PayPal*
Investor-led Growth	While a company's growth positively affects investor attractiveness, the reverse relationship also holds true. New ventures with scalable business models are more likely to attract external funding, leading to accelerated company growth, as suggested by entrepreneurship theory	Stampfl et al. (2013) Dopfer et al. (2017)	Bumper – Bumper's unique service model, which allows customers to spread car repair costs over interest-free monthly repayments, positions it uniquely in the automotive and financial services market. With a network of over 4,000 partners and a recent $48 million Series B funding, the company's plans to grow across Europe, coupled with its impressive track record of 100% increase in gross merchandise value and 80% rise in customer numbers, indicate a robust growth trajectory Investors: Elderstreet Investments, Porsche, Autotech Ventures, InMotion, Shell Ventures, Revo Capital	Focus on business model scalability to increase attractiveness of external funds. *OpenAI*

Velocity-Driven Growth	A strategic approach that prioritises rapid scale and market dominance over initial efficiency or profitability. This is important in markets in which first-mover advantage matters	Kuratko et al. (2020) Hoffman and Yeh (2018)	Travelport – The company recently acquired Deem, a corporate travel management platform, and upgraded over 85% of its agency customers to Travelport+. The new investment will enable further enhancements in Travelport+, including support for a wide range of carrier NDC offerings and the Content Curation Layer, a machine learning-powered search engine. Travelport's path to a $10 billion valuation is anchored in its strong position in the global travel technology sector. Investors: Siris Capital Group, Elliott Investment Management, Davidson Kempner, Canyon Partners Airbnb aggressively expanded its presence worldwide, focussing on improving its service, user experience, and establishing a strong brand in a short timeframe. Entering for first in various geographical markets led Airbnb to a significant first-mover advantage. Top of Form	If the business model is highly scalable and unique, prioritise rapid scale and market dominance over initial efficiency or profitability. Initially, a significant amount of cash will be burned, but later on, the first-mover advantage will lead to a dominant position and high profits. *Airbnb*

Source: Authors' elaboration.

In conclusion, scaling effectively and efficiently often involves leveraging a combination of these growth factors. A platform might start with a product-led approach but then scale up through network effects or an ecosystem strategy. Platforms like Dropbox, Airbnb, and Uber have each used a mix of these strategies. Dropbox utilised network-led growth through referral incentives, Airbnb offered a unique value proposition with a community trust system, and Uber provided a price and convenience advantage over traditional taxis. In addition, growth hacking is a process of continuous experimentation and as such should also support the shift from one category to another based on changes in the market and other endogenous and exogenous factors.

REFERENCES

Acquier, A., Carbone, V., & Massé, D. (2019). How to create value (s) in the sharing economy: Business models, scalability, and sustainability. *Technology Innovation Management Review, 9*(2), 5–24.

Adner, R. (2017). Ecosystem as structure: An actionable construct for strategy. *Journal of Management, 43*(1), 39–58.

Adner, R., & Kapoor, R. (2010). Value creation in innovation ecosystems: How the structure of technological interdependence affects firm performance in new technology generations. *Strategic Management Journal, 31*(3), 306–333.

Ancillai, C., Sabatini, A., Gatti, M., & Perna, A. (2023). Digital technology and business model innovation: A systematic literature review and future research agenda. *Technological Forecasting and Social Change, 188*, 122307.

Ansoff, H. (2007). *Strategic management.* Springer.

Asvanund, A., Clay, K., Krishnan, R., & Smith, M. D. (2004). An empirical analysis of network externalities in peer-to-peer music-sharing networks. *Information Systems Research, 15*(2), 155–174. https://doi.org/10.1287/isre.1040.0020

Bargoni, A., Jabeen, F., Santoro, G., & Ferraris, A. (2023). Growth hacking and international dynamic marketing capabilities: A conceptual framework and research propositions. *International Marketing Review, 41*(1), 74–106. https://doi.org/10.1108/IMR-07-2022-0156

Bargoni, A., Santoro, G., Messeni Petruzzelli, A., & Ferraris, A. (2024). Growth hacking: A critical review to clarify its meaning and guide its practical application. *Technological Forecasting and Social Change, 200*, 123111. https://doi.org/10.1016/j.techfore.2023.123111

Bargoni, A., Smrčka, L., Santoro, G., & Ferraris, A. (2024). Highway to hell or paradise city? Exploring the role of growth hacking in learning from innovation failure. *Technovation, 131*, 102945. https://doi.org/10.1016/j.technovation.2023.102945

Berntzen, M., Hoda, R., Moe, N. B., & Stray, V. (2022). A taxonomy of inter-team coordination mechanisms in large-scale agile. *IEEE Transactions on Software Engineering, 49*(2), 699–718.

Bohnsack, R., & Liesner, M. M. (2019). What the hack? A growth hacking taxonomy and practical applications for firms. *Business Horizons, 62*(6), 799–818. https://doi.org/10.1016/j.bushor.2019.09.001

Bresciani, S., Ferraris, A., & Del Giudice, M. (2018). The management of organizational ambidexterity through alliances in a new context of analysis: Internet of Things (IoT) smart city projects. *Technological Forecasting and Social Change, 136*, 331–338.

Chesbrough, H. (2006). *Open business models: How to thrive in the new innovation landscape*. Harvard Business Press.

Costa Climent, R., & Haftor, D. M. (2021). Value creation through the evolution of business model themes. *Journal of Business Research, 122*, 353–361. https://doi.org/10.1016/j.jbusres.2020.09.007

Cusumano, M. A., Gawer, A., & Yoffie, D. B. (2019). *The business of platforms: Strategy in the age of digital competition, innovation, and power* (Vol. 320). Harper Business New York.

Cusumano, M. A., Gawer, A., Yoffie, D. B., von Bargen, S., & Acquay, K. (2024). The impact of platform business models on the valuations of unicorn companies. *Information and Organization, 34*(3), 100521.

David, P. A., & Greenstein, S. (1990). The economics of compatibility standards: An introduction to recent research. *Economics of Innovation and New Technology, 1*(1–2), 3–41.

Doerr, J. (2018). *Measure what matters: How Google, Bono, and the Gates Foundation rock the world with OKRs*. Penguin.

Dopfer, M., Fallahi, S., Kirchberger, M., & Gassmann, O. (2017). Adapt and strive: How ventures under resource constraints create value through business model adaptations. *Creativity and Innovation Management, 26*(3), 233–246.

Foss, N. J., & Saebi, T. (2017). Fifteen years of research on business model innovation: How far have we come, and where should we go? *Journal of Management, 43*(1), 200–227. https://doi.org/10.1177/0149206316675927

Foss, N. J., & Saebi, T. (2018). Business models and business model innovation: Between wicked and paradigmatic problems. *Long Range Planning, 51*(1), 9–21.

Gaito, R. (2017). *Growth Hacker: Mindset e strumenti per far crescere il tuo business*. FrancoAngeli.

Gawer, A. (2021). Digital platforms' boundaries: The interplay of firm scope, platform sides, and digital interfaces. *Long Range Planning, 54*(5), 102045.

Giustiziero, G., Kretschmer, T., Somaya, D., & Wu, B. (2022). Hyperspecialization and hyperscaling: A resource-based theory of the digital firm. *Strategic Management Journal, 44*, 1391–1424. smj.3365. https://doi.org/10.1002/smj.3365

Graebner, M. E., Eisenhardt, K. M., & Roundy, P. T. (2010). Success and failure in technology acquisitions: Lessons for buyers and sellers. *Academy of Management Perspectives, 24*(3), 73–92.

Gregory, R. W., Henfridsson, O., Kaganer, E., & Kyriakou, H. (2021). The role of artificial intelligence and data network effects for creating user value. *Academy of Management Review, 46*(3), 534–551. https://doi.org/10.5465/amr.2019.0178

Hilbolling, S., Berends, H., Deken, F., & Tuertscher, P. (2020). Complementors as connectors: Managing open innovation around digital product platforms. *R&D Management, 50*(1), 18–30.

Hoffman, R., & Yeh, C. (2018). *Blitzscaling: The lightning-fast path to building massively valuable companies*. Currency.

Holiday, R. (2014). *Growth hacker marketing: A primer on the future of PR, marketing, and advertising*. Penguin.

Husan, R. (1997). The continuing importance of economies of scale in the automotive industry. *European Business Review, 97*(1), 38–42.

Jacobides, M. G. (2019). In the ecosystem economy, what's your strategy? *Harvard Business Review, 97*(5), 128–137.

Johnson, M. W. (2018). *Reinvent your business model: How to seize the white space for transformative growth*. Harvard Business Press.

Kapoor, R., & Agarwal, S. (2017). Sustaining superior performance in business ecosystems: Evidence from application software developers in the iOS and Android smartphone ecosystems. *Organization Science, 28*(3), 531–551.

Keeley, L., Walters, H., Pikkel, R., & Quinn, B. (2013). *Ten types of innovation: The discipline of building breakthroughs*. John Wiley & Sons.

Keller, K. L. (2013). *Strategic brand management: Building, measuring, and managing brand equity* (Global ed.). Pearson.

Kohler, T., Fueller, J., Matzler, K., & Stieger, D. (2011). Co-creation in virtual worlds: The design of the user experience. *MIS Quarterly, 35*(3), 773–788.

Kuratko, D. F., Holt, H. L., & Neubert, E. (2020). Blitzscaling: The good, the bad, and the ugly. *Business Horizons, 63*(1), 109–119.

Maiti, M., Krakovich, V., Shams, S. R., & Vukovic, D. B. (2020). Resource-based model for small innovative enterprises. *Management Decision, 58*(8), 1525–1541.

Markus, M. L. (1987). Toward a "critical mass" theory of interactive media: Universal access, interdependence and diffusion. *Communication Research, 14*(5), 491–511.

Massa, L., Tucci, C. L., & Afuah, A. (2017). A critical assessment of business model research. *Academy of Management Annals, 11*(1), 73–104.

Maurya, A. (2022). *Running lean*. O'Reilly Media, Inc.

McClure, D. (2007). Startup metrics for pirates. *Slideshare. Net*. https://www.slideshare.net/slideshow/startup-metrics-for-pirates-long-version/89026

Moore, J. F. (1993). Predators and prey: A new ecology of competition. *Harvard Business Review, 71*(3), 75–86.

Moro-Visconti, R., Cruz Rambaud, S., & López Pascual, J. (2020). Sustainability in FinTechs: An explanation through business model scalability and market valuation. *Sustainability, 12*(24), 10316. https://doi.org/10.3390/su122410316

Nagle, T. T., & Hogan, J. E. (2006). *The strategy and tactics of pricing: A guide to growing more profitably*. Pearson/Prentice Hall.

Nambisan, S., Siegel, D., & Kenney, M. (2018). On open innovation, platforms, and entrepreneurship. *Strategic Entrepreneurship Journal, 12*(3), 354–368.

Niven, P. R., & Lamorte, B. (2016). *Objectives and key results: Driving focus, alignment, and engagement with OKRs*. John Wiley & Sons.

Osterwalder, A., & Pigneur, Y. (2010). *Business Model Generation: A handbook for visionaries, game changers, and challengers* (Vol. 1). John Wiley & Sons.

Osterwalder, A., Pigneur, Y., Bernarda, G., & Smith, A. (2015). *Value proposition design: How to create products and services customers want*. John Wiley & Sons.

Osterwalder, A., Pigneur, Y., & Clark, T. (2010). *Business Model Generation: A handbook for visionaries, game changers, and challengers*. Wiley.

Ostrom, A. L., Bitner, M. J., Brown, S. W., Burkhard, K. A., Goul, M., Smith-Daniels, V., ... & Rabinovich, E. (2010). Moving forward and making a difference: Research priorities for the science of service. *Journal of Service Research*, 13(1), 4–36.

Parker, G. G., & Van Alstyne, M. W. (2005). Two-sided network effects: A theory of information product design. *Management Science*, 51(10), 1494–1504.

Peltoniemi, M., & Vuori, E. (2004). Business ecosystem as the new approach to complex adaptive business environments. *Proceedings of eBusiness Research Forum*, 2(22), 267–281.

Reischauer, G., Engelmann, A., Gawer, A., & Hoffmann, W. H. (2024). The slipstream strategy: How high-status OEMs coopete with platforms to maintain their digital extensions' edge. *Research Policy*, 53(7), 105032.

Rietveld, J., & Schilling, M. A. (2021). Platform competition: A systematic and interdisciplinary review of the literature. *Journal of Management*, 47(6), 1528–1563.

Ronteau, S., Muzellec, L., Saxena, D., & Trabucchi, D. (2022). *Digital business models: The new value creation and capture mechanisms of the 21st century*. De Gruyter.

Rummel, F., Hüsig, S., & Steinhauser, S. (2022). Two archetypes of business model innovation processes for manufacturing firms in the context of digital transformation. *R&D Management*, 52(4), 685–703.

Sanasi, S. (2023). Entrepreneurial experimentation in business model dynamics: Current understanding and future opportunities. *International Entrepreneurship and Management Journal*, 19(2), 805–836.

Santoro, G. (2019). *Beyond Strategy: How to Compete in Dynamic Business Environments*. Giappichelli.

Santoro, G., Bresciani, S., & Papa, A. (2020). Collaborative modes with cultural and creative industries and innovation performance: The moderating role of heterogeneous sources of knowledge and absorptive capacity. *Technovation*, 92, 102040.

Saura, J. R., Palacios-Marqués, D., & Ribeiro-Soriano, D. (2022). Exploring the boundaries of open innovation: Evidence from social media mining. *Technovation*, 119, 102447.

Sedera, D., Lokuge, S., Grover, V., Sarker, S., & Sarker, S. (2016). Innovating with enterprise systems and digital platforms: A contingent resource-based theory view. *Information & Management*, *53*(3), 366–379.

Shapiro, C., & Varian, H. R. (2010). *Information rules: A strategic guide to the network economy* (Nachdr.). Harvard Business School Press.

Silva, D. S., Ghezzi, A., Aguiar, R. B. de, Cortimiglia, M. N., & ten Caten, C. S. (2020). Lean startup, Agile methodologies and customer development for business model innovation: A systematic review and research agenda. *International Journal of Entrepreneurial Behavior & Research*, *26*(4), 595–628.

Spieth, P., Schneckenberg, D., & Ricart, J. E. (2014). Business model innovation – State of the art and future challenges for the field. *R&D Management*, *44*(3), 237–247.

Stampfl, G., Prügl, R., & Osterloh, V. (2013). An explorative model of business model scalability. *International Journal of Product Development*, *18*(3–4), 226–248.

Stummer, C., Kundisch, D., & Decker, R. (2018). Platform launch strategies. *Business & Information Systems Engineering*, *60*, 167–173.

Täuscher, K., & Abdelkafi, N. (2018). Scalability and robustness of business models for sustainability: A simulation experiment. *Journal of Cleaner Production*, *170*, 654–664.

Täuscher, K., & Laudien, S. M. (2018). Understanding platform business models: A mixed methods study of marketplaces. *European Management Journal*, *36*(3), 319–329.

Teece, D. J. (2010). Business models, business strategy and innovation. *Long Range Planning*, *43*(2–3), 172–194. https://doi.org/10.1016/j.lrp.2009.07.003

Troisi, O., Maione, G., Grimaldi, M., & Loia, F. (2020). Growth hacking: Insights on data-driven decision-making from three firms. *Industrial Marketing Management*, *90*, 538–557. https://doi.org/10.1016/j.indmarman.2019.08.005

Varga, S., Cholakova, M., Jansen, J. J., Mom, T. J., & Kok, G. J. (2023). From platform growth to platform scaling: The role of decision rules and network effects over time. *Journal of Business Venturing*, *38*(6), 106346.

Weinberg, G., & Mares, J. (2015). *Traction: How any startup can achieve explosive customer growth*. Portfolio.

Wirtz, B. W., Schilke, O., & Ullrich, S. (2010). Strategic development of business models: Implications of the Web 2.0 for creating value on the internet. *Long Range Planning, 43*(2–3), 272–290.

Wodtke, C. (2016). *Radical focus: Achieving your most important goals with objectives and key results*. cwodtke.com

Xie, X., & Wang, H. (2020). How can open innovation ecosystem modes push product innovation forward? An fsQCA analysis. *Journal of Business Research, 108*, 29–41.

Zott, C., Amit, R., & Massa, L. (2011). The business model: Recent developments and future research. *Journal of Management, 37*(4), 1019–1042.

Printed and bound by CPI Group (UK) Ltd, Croydon, CR0 4YY
30/10/2024

14583848-0003